The inside story of the al-Hilli murders

TOM PARRY

Mirror Books

Published by Mirror Books,
an imprint of Trinity Mirror plc,
1 Canada Square,
London E14 5AP, England

www.mirrorbooks.com
twitter.com/themirrorbooks

Mirror Books Editor: Hanna Tavner
Design: Paul Mason and Susan Topping
Editor: Daniel Bourke

ISBN 978-1-907324-59-8

Printed and bound in Great Britain by CPI Group (UK) Ltd,
Croydon, CR0 4YY

For my ever supportive wife, Katia
and sons, Louis and Remy

ACKNOWLEDGEMENTS

I would like to thank many people for their help in researching the background of the victims of the Chevaline murders.

They include Saad's friends Dr Zaid Alabdi, James Mathews and Gary Aked, his accountant Julian Steadman and his close neighbour Jack Saltman.

Judith Weatherly has been extremely forthcoming in providing background on Iqbal al-Hilli from her time in the United States.

In France Eric Maillaud and Stephane Bouchet gave me considerable insight into the progress of the case. Stephane Bouchet from the Dauphiné Libéré newspaper put me in touch with several interested parties. Many other people in the Annecy region gave their time willingly. Lars Gardenius also provided useful background material.

I would like to thank Professor David Wilson from the University of Birmingham for his expertise in analysing the specific characteristics of these murders.

Thanks also to my Daily Mirror colleagues Vicky Smith and Ben Rossington as well as Linda Phillips for Swedish translation help and Nathalie Rothschild in Stockholm.

Finally, I wish to acknowledge Fergus McKenna, Hanna Tavner and Daniel Bourke for helping to bring this book to fruition.

Tom Parry

CONTENTS

Chapter 1

A bloodbath in the Alpine forest

Off a minor Alpine mountain road, hemmed in by the shadows of a dense forest, a maroon estate car is backed into a bank of earth with its rear wheels spinning. A desperate wheezing comes from the revving engine. Exhaust, burning rubber and oil fumes drift through the pines above the parking bay.

Across the road an expensive racing bike lies flat.

As if from nowhere a young girl, her hair matted with blood, stumbles hunched on to the road. Dressed in a thin T-shirt, black shorts and sandals, she stumbles on to her side then lies prone in front of the revving car. She occasionally lets go an agonised cry as she slips in and out of consciousness.

To her left, the form of a middle-aged cyclist can be made out. He is inert, perfectly still, on his back.

It becomes obvious the athletic man in white cycling shirt and black cycling shorts is not breathing. His injuries were not caused by some prang on his steep ascent to this remote lay-by above Lake Annecy, Haute-Savoie, France. He has been shot repeatedly and the gravel to his left is stained with his blood.

The BMW's windows are peppered with bullet-holes. The polished paintwork is smudged by dust but otherwise pristine.

Inside are the bodies of three adults, slumped forward. Their faces are obscured, but they look Middle Eastern. In the driver's seat is a man, his grey-haired head on the steering wheel. He wears a cobalt blue polo shirt and jeans and he has two bullet wounds to his forehead. A thick clot of blood trickles from one of them down his limp form in a claret as rich as the paint of the car.

In the back seat are two women, shot in the head. The older one's headscarf is smothered in blood. The other's shoulder-length dark hair is dyed auburn at the crown. She wears a shortsleeved black summer top, and her light blue long skirt covers the foot-well.

They are not dressed for an arduous hike. The

lay-by, called Le Martinet, is usually frequented by hunters and well-equipped summer hikers, some heading off for days in the wilderness. A green board at the other end displays a map of walking routes.

There are no signs of resistance from the victims of this conflict-zone carnage other than the tyre marks that sweep a semi-oval across the clearing.

There is no sign of an assassin, a getaway vehicle or an abandoned gun. The mountain birds, their song briefly quelled by the uproarious violence, reclaim their territory by cooing and flitting around the forest canopy. The warm sun almost directly overhead starts to dry the blood that marks the ground. The air above the forest is pregnant with the first witness' questions.

What has happened here? Who did this? And why?

Questions the world is asking still.

Chapter 2

Chevaline: Horror on our doorstep

They call places like Chevaline "la France profonde" – deepest France. It is picture-postcard France, the kind of place you could visit 20 years apart and nothing would have changed.

At 3.30pm on Wednesday, September 5, 2012, the 206 residents were blessed with hot late summer sunshine. The sky was perfect cyan, artfully daubed with a few harmless cirrus clouds, and barely a puff of wind stirred the trees. A smudge of mist that had at dawn obscured Lake Annecy below had been simmered away. Gone too were most of the season's tourists, who pass through the village in search of Alpine vistas. The local children were back at school and quiet life was being restored to this idyllic hamlet. Those fortunate enough to live here, untroubled by the need to return to offices in Paris, Geneva, Lyon or London, could pause from their tasks to gaze down on a green and blue panorama as magnificent as any in the cherished Haute-Savoie region.

The temperature hit 30C. It was an afternoon that made you feel lucky to be alive.

Chevaline is a few kilometres off the Route d'Annecy, which skirts the western banks of one of the most visited and picturesque freshwater lakes in the French Alps. The village has no restaurants, no bar, no supermarket; it is too small to even merit a bakers or a butchers. For a long time it was the smallest village in its administrative area. Its population declined for most of the century. Saint Martin's, its 17th century church, is infrequently used. Only in the past few decades did newcomers arrive, attracted by the views across the Faverges valley.

Chevaline is so incidental that when you look it up on Google Maps, a horse butcher in Paris comes up. The adjective "chevaline" describes everything equine, including horsemeat. They think the village got its name because it was used as a garrison for Roman cavalry.

Aside from the occasional rattle of a tractor, nothing much breaks the peace here. It is, literally, above the normal troubles of modern life: the mayor's domain is all higher than 1,000m altitude.

But at some time roughly between 3.35pm and 3.45pm on that drowsy afternoon, Chevaline's carefully managed tranquillity would be disturbed in the most violent way imaginable. From that moment it would be the place where one of the most extraordinary crimes of recent times took place. Chevaline has become the notorious location for a mystery so seemingly impossible to fathom that its most prominent investigator, Annecy state prosecutor Eric Maillaud, has called it: "the perfect crime".

When he made that remark in September 2014 – the two-year anniversary of the massacre – Monsieur Maillaud was not paying a compliment to the perpetrator or trying to be insensitive to the victims. He was expressing frustration that he and a huge team of French and British detectives, lawyers, forensic scientists and criminal behaviourists have failed to establish a line of inquiry which properly explains what is known locally as "la tuerie de Chevaline" – the Chevaline massacre.

Chevaline's mayor at the time, Didier Berthollet, was hiking when the murders took place. He returned to a village besieged by police officers as ambulances sped through to the clearing, three kilometres away. He provided officers with a map of the sparsely populated area.

"We have never seen such horror on our doorstep," Monsieur Berthollet said to journalists the following day. "We are stunned. It's surreal that this has happened in our very quiet village. All of us are very surprised. Nothing happens in this village. There is nothing here, only about 150 inhabitants and 300 cows."

No one in Chevaline will ever forget Wednesday, September 5, 2012.

That afternoon, Iraqi-born British engineer Saad al-Hilli and his family had got into his maroon BMW estate at the Solitaire du Lac campsite on the shores of Lake Annecy. The car, cared for by Saad as though it were a child, was parked alongside the equally cherished family caravan. The family had been there since the Monday two nights before.

The family was Saad, 50, his wife Iqbal, 47, also born in Baghdad, two gorgeous daughters Zainab, seven, and Zeena, four, and Iqbal's mum, Suhaila al-Allaf, 74.

The girls helped Suhaila clamber into the back seat. Zainab was allowed to sit in the front because looking through the front window made her less carsick.

The campsite is in Saint Jorioz, about nine miles from Chevaline. The al-Hillis had been at a site just around the corner, Village Camping Europa, for two nights following their arrival in the region late on Saturday. The two are 1.6 miles apart, a five-minute drive through the lakeside town. A Dutch family pitched next to the al-Hilli family at the Europa site claimed the Brits had intended to stay the whole week but moved in a hurry. The campsite owner claims not.

The Dutch tourists described a man dressed in a suit lurking around the al-Hilli caravan there. He had, they said, a "Balkans" appearance. After a "heated conversation" with Saad, the man tapped on the car bonnet with his hand and disappeared. He has never been traced.

Other campers claimed Saad left the Europa site up to five times a day, alone in his car.

The family had taken the 10pm sailing from Dover to Calais the previous Wednesday, August 29. They spent three slow days travelling the eight hours to Annecy, going west to Rouen, three hours from Calais, instead of driving straight through eastern France. They spent their first night at Vert-en-Drouais near the city of Dreux to the west of Paris. Next they stayed at the municipal site in picturesque riverside La Charité-sur-Loire in the Nievre region south of the capital. Nothing suspicious occurred during the journey. In La Charité, Saad bought some cable ties to reinforce the caravan tow bracket. They had a return ticket for Friday, September 7.

This was their second summer in a row caravanning in France. The previous year Saad had gleefully sent pictures back to his friends to show what a great time they were having.

To anyone who met them, the al-Hillis seemed a normal British suburban family enjoying a normal family holiday. Solitaire du Lac offers plenty of distractions for children and has its own restaurant and playground. Pitches are grassy, flat and spacious, big enough for Saad to have enjoyed a game of badminton; a sport he once said was his favourite. The site has its "feet in the clear waters of the lake", boast the owners. Campers can walk down a track to the sandy banks to swim or canoe. Saad pitched a three-man dome tent and extended a large canvas awning on the caravan's side. They had everything they needed to cook and they had bikes to get about locally.

Why then on a beautiful afternoon would they drive up a mountain road to a place that had no views and from which, unless you are physically able and kitted out to go hiking or mountain-biking, you can only turn back? It seems unlikely Zeena, who still liked to be carried by her dad, and retired teacher Suhaila would have wanted to set off on an endurance march from Le Martinet.

Saad was behind the wheel when they set off around 2.30pm. The engineer, from the leafy commuter town of Claygate, Surrey, always drove. It was for him not a chore but a pleasure, an intrinsic part of the holiday experience. Iqbal, in contrast, didn't like driving even around Claygate. Saad bought her a car after she joined him to get married in Britain in 2003 but it sat on the driveway for years.

The al-Hillis might have enjoyed a typically long French lunch, finished off by fresh bread and cheese. It would have been a lovely afternoon for a snooze or a dip. Instead they took the BMW out.

Next to Saad, in the passenger seat of the diesel, was his eldest Zainab. Although in a child's car seat, she should under French law really have been in the back. She should also have been at school that week. Her Year 3 classmates had returned the day before and met their new teacher. But like most children given the opportunity to miss lessons, Zainab was happy. What a treat to be running around a campsite in the sun with her sister instead of sitting at a desk in her school uniform.

"They were a nice, normal family," said Dutch tourist Sandy Rambout, who was camped close to Saad's caravan. "The kids were playing outside the caravan."

Another camper said she had seen the two girls collecting apples with their mum and grandmother.

In the back seat on the right was Suhaila. Apparently still very active despite her advancing years, she regularly accompanied her daughter on excursions to the Continent and in Britain. A retired English teacher based in Sweden but educated in Surrey, Suhaila had been a widow since husband Abdul al-Saffar had died from kidney problems the previous year. Although surrounded by other family in Stockholm, friends believe she missed the company of Iqbal and was eager to join their French trip. Saad picked her up from Iqbal's sister Fadwa's home in Berkshire the day they sailed. Fadwa was a PhD student at University. Suhaila liked England too having studied in London for a PhD in biology in the 1970s. One relative described how she "longed" to spend more time with her grandchildren.

Beside Suhaila was Zeena, Saad and Iqbal's youngest, who was due to start at school in a few weeks. A playful and cute child, she made friends wherever the family went. At the campsite Saad was teaching Zeena to ride a bike, Ms Rambout said. The doting dad also clipped a two-wheel trailer to the end of the tandem he rode with Iqbal for the girls to sit on.

Iqbal sat in the rear on the left. She would have had the best view back over the valley as the car went through Doussard, a slightly larger settlement, and through Chevaline. She might have glimpsed first-time para-gliders tandem-jumping off the Col de la Forclaz over the lake.

No one paid much notice to the British BMW pulling out of Le Solitaire du Lac. The distinctive car, unwieldy on the narrow circuit around the site, would have turned left and travelled down the D1508 encircling the lake. The left bank, where the al-Hilli family were camped, is the most popular so the road gets clogged. After leaving Saint Jorioz they would have followed the shoreline before reaching a fork at Doussard. If they had turned left they would have crossed the marshy reserve at the mouth of the lake and the right bank would have taken them to the city of Annecy. But the al-Hillis continued on through Doussard.

There are no CCTV cameras on this stretch of road, nothing to show the BMW or its occupants on their short journey.

Three dated and timed photographs survived on Suhaila's camera showing the al-Hillis in Doussard at exactly 3.15pm. The family pose happily. Saad is back left with his arms around Zainab. Iqbal, back right, clutches Zeena in her arms as the little girl cranes her head around to look at the camera. They are in front of a stone building beside a fast-flowing stream. Another image is said to show Saad with one of his daughters on his shoulders. In a snap taken by Saad, Suhaila smiles.

3.15pm was precisely 33 minutes before the first person on the scene at Le Martinet tried to call for an ambulance on his mobile.

The drive between the spot where the picture was taken in Doussard and the crime scene takes around 12 minutes. The time window during which the killer could have shot his victims can be narrowed probably to less than ten minutes.

One person to notice the maroon BMW that afternoon was builder Laurent Fillion-Robin. Laurent, 40, was working at the last house in Chevaline before the remote single-track Combe d'Ire forest road begins.

"I saw an English car coming up the road from the village," he recalled when he was interviewed in the days after the massacre. "There were no other cars with it. I did not see or hear any other cars pass that afternoon.

"I didn't hear any shooting," Laurent continued. "You do hear shooting from the hunters sometimes but I didn't hear anything that afternoon. Perhaps they had a silencer."

Like everyone in Chevaline, Laurent remains baffled by Saad's journey to that lay-by in the middle of the afternoon. Incorrectly described as a beauty spot in many of the initial news stories, this small and insignificant clearing is not really somewhere you would go unless you had a specific reason. It is a base camp, not a panoramic beauty spot.

"It is not the sort of place families with young children or older people would go to," Laurent has confirmed.

The tortuous single track to Le Martinet is called the Route Forestière Domaniale de la Combe d'Ire. The road was built to bring charcoal down from the forest in the 1930s. Without some local knowledge, you wouldn't know it was there.

The BMW passed a brown sign on the right indicating the start of the forest route. A white panel below indicates in French, English and German that this is a "dangerous road" on which driving is prohibited three kilometres further. To the left is an agricultural barn where local trees are processed into planks. It is full of redundant agricultural equipment. The kind of place, I have come to know, that would have fascinated Saad, an incorrigible collector of old machines, lawnmowers and vehicle parts.

After leaving Chevaline the road enters dense woodland, with the mountains only occasionally visible ahead. In some places logs ready for collection are stacked by the roadside. For most of the route the Ire river is to the left, shielded behind a wall of fir, oak and beech. Afterwards the river is crossed and recrossed in a series of iron-railed bridges. The sound as white water tumbles over stony chutes maybe helps explain why no one heard any shots.

The family passed several other lay-bys before Le Martinet. One can imagine Saad reflecting he would have enjoyed cycling this way himself – he enjoyed bike rides through the woods of Surrey and Sussex as a younger man. One can also imagine the little girls in the back complaining they were bored.

At Le Martinet, there were no other day-trippers. A red-ringed sign indicates the track beyond is for residents and forestry workers only. It is hard to believe the al-Hillis ever intended to proceed further than the parking bay. Perhaps, as one family friend suggested to me, Saad had taken a wrong turn and paused only for Zainab to get out and go to the toilet.

For those not intending to hike, it is a place to maybe take a few snaps of the foliage then spin back around. For the al-Hillis it was a place of no return.

Chapter 3

First on the scene: the British cyclist

Former RAF pilot Brett Martin looked out of the window of his holiday home near Lake Annecy and decided it was a fine day for a strenuous cycle ride. He had spent the morning doing jobs around the house in Lathuile, the small village between the lake and Chevaline where the now 55-year-old had bought a house several years before. Brett, whose full name is William Brett Martin, got into the saddle at about 2.30pm, roughly the same time the al-Hilli family left their Solitaire du Lac campsite just down the road. He had no particular route in mind. He was in France without his family, so had no need to be back for a set time.

After he rode through Chevaline, another bicycle overtook Brett. Although a decent rider, Brett was no match for this cyclist who would turn out to be Sylvain Mollier, the 45-year-old local man shot dead to the side of the al-Hillis' car.

In an interview with the BBC the week after the murders, Brett, from Brighton, recalled what he encountered when he got to the lay-by. He agreed that what he saw that day would never leave him. It was, Brett said in a very understated British way, "the sort of thing you never in your life expect to come across and rather unpleasant of course".

Brett, who spends the rest of his time at his home on the English South Coast with his wife Theresa, 54, has done his best to move on, but one can imagine rarely a day goes by without his thinking of the shooting.

"As I approached the scene, the first thing I saw was a bike on its side," he recalled in that interview. "I'd seen the cyclist ahead of me much earlier so I thought he was just having a rest. As I got a little bit closer, a very young child stumbled out on to the road and at first I thought she was just playing, for she looked from a distance like she was sort of falling over, larking about, like a child would. However, as I approached her, it was obvious that she was quite badly injured and there was a lot of blood on her."

That child was Zainab al-Hilli. Zainab, who just a few hours before had been playing with other children at the campsite, had been shot once in the shoulder and her skull had been badly fractured from "repeated blows" by a blunt instrument. It was later revealed she had been beaten "very badly" by the butt of the Luger – pistol-whipped.

"I then saw the car with its engine revving and wheels spinning," Brett continued. "It seemed at that moment there had been a terrible car accident."

Still bewildered by the shocking scene that confronted him, Brett focused on the girl, using his RAF first-aid training and his cool head. French police later complimented his ability to remain calm in a moment of extraordinary pressure. Though Brett to this day rejects the notion that he was a hero, it is entirely possible that Zainab owes him her life. He was pleased to find the seven-year-old was breathing but she was covered in blood and had some obvious, very severe head injuries.

"She was prone on the road, moaning, semi-conscious," Brett went on. "And she was lying in front of the car with its wheels spinning. So my immediate thought was that she needed to be moved in case the car lurched forward and ran her over. So I gently attended to her and moved her into a position clear of where the vehicle could possibly go, clear of the road, and put her in a recovery position as best I could and asked her to stay there and then moved on."

He moved to the cyclist on the ground. The immobile form of French dad-of-three Sylvain was some distance from his bike. Sylvain's legs and arms were not grazed or cut in the way someone would be if they had suffered a bike fall, Brett saw. He carefully moved Sylvain's body away from the car – which still looked like it might suddenly lurch forward – and then checked for a pulse.

Brett says: "It seemed to me like he was probably dead. I couldn't feel a pulse and the most obvious thing was the totally inanimate body, so I moved on from him now he was away from the car. I thought it's probably a good idea because I could smell burning rubber and that sort of hot burning engine smell."

The next priority was to switch off the engine, but the car doors were all locked.

"I needed to break the window to get in," he explained during the interview, adding, "I noticed there were some holes and I was starting to think, 'Is that a bullet hole?' as I was breaking the window. I had my cycle gloves on. I literally pushed the window in because it was already cracked."

With the drone of the engine quieted, Brett could take stock of the people inside the car.

Looking at their injuries, he felt sure what had happened to them could not be the result of a bad manoeuvre in the road by the driver, or a head-on smash with the cyclist. As he described the scene in the interview, he stopped mid-flow, reliving what must have been the most traumatic moment of his life.

"I have never seen people who have been shot before, for real – more the Hollywood stuff, but actually it seemed to be just like a Hollywood scene and if someone had said 'cut' and everybody got up and walked away, that would have been it," he explained. "But unfortunately it was real life… it became quite obvious now, taking stock, that it was a gun crime. Now, I was getting a little bit anxious because I thought perhaps there's some crazy person in the woods… I started scanning the woods to see whether there was some nutter, who knows what, with a gun, and I was going to be the next shot. Was it some sort of hunter with a high-powered rifle shooting from a distance or what?"

Asked to describe the condition of the bodies in more vivid detail, Brett said: "There was a lot of blood and heads with bullet-holes in them."

Saad al-Hilli, Iqbal al-Hilli and Suhaila al-Allaf were totally inanimate. All of them had been shot in the head at point-blank range. They must have died instantly.

He tried to call the emergency services on his mobile but there was no signal. Should he stay to tend to the girl who was breathing but unconscious, or go back down the hill to the village to get help, leaving her to who knows what fate? Or should he take her with him?

"She was very light," he explained. "So I could have done a sort of fireman's lift and taken her down on my bike, but she had a lot of injuries and it seems from the low level of medical training that I've had over the years that if there's a risk of internal bleeding, wounds, things like that, sort of dragging her like a rag doll over my shoulder might have perhaps killed her so the prudent thing was to leave her in the recovery position and go for help on my bike as soon and as fast as I could."

Brett, a father himself, admitted it "wasn't a very comfortable decision".

Fortunately for Zainab, apparently the only person who could still be helped, Brett met a car about four hundred yards down the road.

Inside the car were a man and two women, hikers heading to the clearing to park the car. Brett managed to explain in broken French that something terrible had happened further up. The driver, Philippe, then 41, drove up to the clearing. Brett followed behind, tentatively.

"He was in a panic," Philippe recounted to French newspaper Le Parisien. "He explained to me with difficulty in bad French that there had been a drama a little higher up. He wanted to alert the emergency services. I wasn't sure whether he didn't have a mobile telephone or he couldn't get a signal up there."

When they got there, the driver immediately suspected Brett, assuming he must have had something to do with the awful scene.

"I linked the English plates on the car with the Englishman I was standing next to and thought the worst," Philippe said in a TV documentary recorded a year after the events. "I went to punch him… he shouted, 'It's not me! It's not me!'"

After reaching the murder scene, and realising Brett was not involved, Philippe turned his car around, facing downhill, in case they needed to make a quick getaway. He was horrified by the macabre stillness of the scene, as though the bodies were actors playing dead for a movie director. Philippe was close enough to say the bullet-hole in Saad's head was as big as a coin. Philippe claims it was obvious there was "nothing more to be done" when he saw the car.

The hikers got a signal on their phones and raised the alarm.

Three fire service trucks and an ambulance were the first to arrive at the site, which was soon cordoned off as a crime scene. No one knew where the killer was, but the unarmed firefighters worked without concern for their own safety.

Police took lengthy statements from Brett, Philippe and his two companions but did not touch the car for fear of disturbing any evidence. Brett says his initial interview lasted six hours and he returned to the scene the following weekend to "fill the gaps" in his account. When he later went back he was given a bullet-proof vest to wear. The French investigators were taking no chances.

If the murderer was lurking somewhere in the forest, he would conclude that after Zainab, who was still clinging on to life, Brett was the only person with potentially useful clues to identify him.

Police wanted to build a timeline of precisely when the killer struck. It will never be possible to determine the precise moment the bullets were fired, but thanks to Brett they were able to narrow it down to a brief window.

Speaking the week after the massacre, Brett

admitted he was clueless as to what lay behind the mysterious murders.

"I have no idea what actually happened," he said, "like probably the rest of the world. I'm very curious to know and would very much like the perpetrators to be brought to book... to do something quite so savage and to brutalise a young child as they did is not very pleasant, so they're obviously pretty unpleasant people who perpetrated this."More than two years after the Chevaline

massacre, Brett still does not like to give too much away about his personal life. He knows that if a killer were ever brought to justice his own testimony might be crucial to gaining a conviction. And given what he witnessed that day, whoever did it is not someone by whom he would like to be targeted.

Prosecutor Eric Maillaud, speaking several days after the attack, said Brett "should be congratulated for his swift actions".

But back on the day of the murders one more

astonishing dramatic twist was to come.

As the emergency services took control of the scene, just a few feet away, inside the car, a small heart was still beating. Unseen and unheard for eight hours was four-year-old Zeena, cowering under her dead mother's flowing skirt in the footwell of the back seat.

Chapter 4

An alarming discovery

For Prosecutor Eric Maillaud, the day started normally. There was paperwork to be completed, meetings to be taken, phone calls to be made and decisions about prosecution cases to be finalised. And then, mid-afternoon, he took a call that would change his life.

"The officers at the scene knew immediately it would be a murder inquiry and called my colleague, the magistrate on call," he said. "He called me and we went up there."

As he sped up the mountain track just the other end of the lake from his office he had only the bare facts. There were bodies in a car and the body of a French cyclist on the ground. An air ambulance had been called to fly Zainab to Grenoble Hospital for emergency treatment.

The succinct briefing was no preparation for

the grisly scene that faced Monsieur le Procureur.

"I could see very little at first," he told me. "I could just about make out the vague outlines of the bodies in the car. A crime scene is frozen; we cannot approach the victims. The only thing I could see was the BMW estate car stuck into the mountain and then the bike and the French cyclist a little bit in front and to the right of the vehicle. It was starting to get dark, night was falling; this was autumn. When I got up there it must have been around 5pm. We could only guess at what had happened."

Asked if he was shocked by the scene, Mr Maillaud answered frankly: "I should say both yes and no, and that is not because of callousness on my part. It is like asking a surgeon to think differently about the patients he operates on. For me, this had to be treated simply as a murder, like any other murder. Of course, there is some emotion when you see something like that, but one tries to keep it in check.

"I was most affected by what had happened to the daughter, to Zainab, but then I had to do my job. If you are overcome by emotions, you cannot. I had to get on with it, notwithstanding the fact that it was extremely rare for there to be so many victims, particularly here. In the region of Haute-Savoie there are crimes, there are murders, but rarely several people at the same time, rarely a whole family. All of us - myself, the gendarmes, the other magistrate - we all had the impression we were dealing with something unique."

But just how unusual events would prove to be was not immediately apparent in those first moments.

"It could have been a situation in which one family had killed another and the whole thing had been solved in 48 hours," Monsieur Maillaud added. "Things might have followed more straightforwardly. But that is not the case."

About the time the prosecutor was familiarising himself with the scene, I and hundreds of other foreign journalists were being sent on our way to Annecy.

As I left the Daily Mirror offices in Canary Wharf, Sky News was flashing updates that a British-Iraqi family had been shot in the Alps. I had at first thought this might be a story in which everything would be wrapped up quickly. The perpetrator, probably a local gun-nut psychotic, would be rounded up within hours and the family, maybe newly arrived in the

UK, would be barely known in Surrey.

All this time, Zeena remained undiscovered, cowering under the back seat. The Annecy and Chambéry police had made the fateful decision to wait for forensic experts from the specialist police criminal research unit, the IRCGN, to arrive from Paris before they properly examined the car. There was no movement at the scene so therefore no need to disturb what would be absolutely crucial evidence until the forensic specialists got there, they surmised. The only person to have any contact with the bodies was a doctor, wearing full forensic overalls, whose primary duty was to establish that all the victims were definitely dead.

Local forensic officers took fingerprint swabs from the outside of the vehicle, carefully making sure not to apply pressure to the cracked windows so the bullet holes could be examined intact by the ballistics experts. They located the spent bullets embedded in the road surface, and they carefully scoured the surroundings, doing their utmost not to tread on any strange object which might provide a clue later on. But for anything more they resolutely waited for the guys with the real expertise to get down from the capital.

The local officers had incorrectly deduced that the three dead adults in the car and the badly injured Zainab were the only members of the al-Hilli family. A helicopter equipped with thermal imaging cameras had flown over the BMW, and had failed to detect any trace of life. The dead bodies would still have been emitting some heat; it was therefore assumed the search was at an end.

"When the officers got there what they saw in addition to the bodies was one single child's seat," Monsieur Maillaud explained to me during a recent lengthy interview. "Outside they had found one little girl. One child seat equals one child. If there had been another seat they might have thought differently, but nothing enabled us to think there was another child. No one knew this family, they were foreign; there was no quick way for us to establish they had a second child. A helicopter passed over the car with a heat detector. It showed colours compatible with the dead adults' bodies relatively quickly. It did not detect a different colour that would have indicated someone being alive."

Only after interviewing some of the al-Hilli family's campsite neighbours at the Solitaire du Lac did the gendarmes establish that there was another child, a little girl, who was nowhere to be seen. Her name, one of the campers said, was Zeena. Confronted by this unexpected development, officers down at the campsite made an urgent call to their colleagues instructing them to re-examine the back of the car. There was a missing child.

It was not until shortly before midnight that the forensic team finally took the decision to re-check the vehicle.

And there, at last, was four-year-old Zeena.

Stock still, crouched down, absolutely frozen in fear, her breaths quiet in case the gunman was still around. Uncertain whether the foreign voices she had been hearing in the long hours since the gunshots were friendly or not, little Zeena hadn't called out. She hadn't moved an inch. She was under her mother's and grandmother's skirts. Perhaps she clung to her mum's familiar, comforting body, even as it became cold and immobile. Maybe she whispered for her mummy and daddy in the silence that followed the terrifying blasts, imploring them to wake up. The scent of her mum's perfume, so familiar her whole life, must have been a reassurance.

As the petite little girl crawled out from beneath her dead mother's body, so dazed and confused that she did not realise the inert form still in the car was her beloved mother, the police officers involved were visibly stunned. They had never witnessed anything like this.

As Zeena was taken to safety, comforted by family liaison officers and social workers, the full probe of the scene began at last.

When I landed at nearby Geneva Airport in Switzerland in the early hours of September 6, I had a message on my mobile from my newsdesk in London informing me of the incredible news about Zeena. It was a staggering development in a story that was becoming harder to interpret by the second. I headed straight for the first press conference.

Inside the large hall at the Annecy Palais de Justice, Monsieur Maillaud sat at the front with gendarme Lieutenant-Colonel Vinnemann, both looking exhausted.

"Zeena was hidden under the bodies for some eight hours and didn't move for the whole time," Monsieur Maillaud explained to the packed room of reporters. "She remained prostrate beneath the skirts of her loved ones in a jumble of bags for nearly eight hours. She could not tell the difference between the good guys and the bad guys. She spontaneously began to smile and speak in English when the gendarme took her in his arms and pulled her out of the car. She had heard the noises, the cries, but couldn't say more."

Lt Col Vinnemann seemed to downplay what Zeena had gone through. "She said she had heard some noise and hid," he told reporters. "She smiled with relief as she was found. She said, 'Where is mummy? I want my mummy.'"

Monsieur Maillaud confirmed: "She is not fully aware of the magnitude of what happened or the consequences for her."

It was left to Vinnemann to defend the decision not to look for Zeena earlier. "We were not looking for survivors because all the evidence was that there was no one else involved," he said. "The car window had been hit by a bullet and if we had opened the door, the window would have collapsed and we would have lost vital ballistic evidence."

Monsieur Maillaud was clearly already exasperated by the sheer number and array of questions, and it was still less than 24 hours since the crime.

To the local media, he was a well-known figure. The role of prosecutor in France is very different to that of a Crown Prosecution Service lawyer in the UK. Rather than being someone in an office who makes a decision on a prosecution once the police have gathered their evidence, a prosecutor in France is the public face of a criminal investigation. He works alongside the police from the moment a crime is reported, steering their inquiries in a particular direction. Although it is down to the police to interview suspects, gather forensic evidence and carry out surveillance, the prosecutor oversees their movements. It is a much more hands-on role, and sometimes a political role too. Prosecutors do not simply present the police's case to the court when it comes to trial.

When the Chevaline killings happened, this previously unobtrusive legal figure was suddenly thrust on to the world stage. It was unlike anything he had ever experienced, a career-defining case. Yet he talked to the world's press as if they all worked at the local newspaper, Le Dauphiné Libéré, little thinking that every unguarded phrase he uttered would be analysed in London, in Sydney, in New York and in Baghdad. This career lawyer who had previously worked mostly on cases with only regional importance was like a rabbit in the headlights as he spoke into the microphones of hundreds of international TV news networks.

The son of two doctors from the Sarthe region in north-west France, Maillaud was highly experienced. After studying as a magistrate in Bordeaux, he had steadily worked his way through the French court hierarchy, taking posts across the country. Prior to his appointment in Annecy, he had worked for seven years in Libourne, near the famous vineyards of St Emilion and Pomerol.

Getting the posting in upmarket Annecy would be a big deal to any French lawyer, the culmination of a career.

When I arrived there in early September 2012, the sun-loungers on the Impérial Beach a short walk from the Palais de Justice were all still in use in the late summer sun. Children swam to the diving platform in the centre of the lake. Elegant, well-heeled women in Grace Kelly sunglasses walked their perfectly groomed terriers and Dachshunds on the banks of the lake. At café tables in the shadow of the Palais de Justice they sipped mid-morning coffees, taking posers' drags on cigarettes. Swimwear models married to wealthy Geneva bankers whiled away the hours waiting for their husbands to return from their offices an hour over the border in the mega-rich enclave of Talloires. Cyclists did laps around the 15-kilometre serpent-shaped lake.

For many the attractions of the lake are more appealing than the French Riviera, about five or six hours further south. The crowds are less intense, the sand is grainier, the water is fresh, not salty, and the temperatures in July and August are more bearable. Medieval buildings cluster around narrow cobbled lanes leading off from Venetian-style bridges over frothing emerald-green waterways. The city is one of the playgrounds of the European elite: an idyllic spot, where the still, crystal-clear waters are always inviting, where the restaurants along the canals provide a panoply of gastronomic choices, and where little happens to dislodge the feeling of privilege that most have paid handsomely for.

You can see the shimmering lake from Monsieur Maillaud's office in the Palais de Justice, where we met for the extensive interview for this book. Through the tree-line, the snow-crested tops of the mountains were visible.

At his desk, he stoutly defended the caution his investigative team exercised that first day. Nearly three years afterwards, he still pondered the laborious process, and whether Zeena could have been found any quicker.

"I have often asked myself about little Zeena being hidden in the back for eight hours, as have the investigators too, of course," he conceded. "When you get to a motorway accident with lots of people dead, lots of fog, and lots of vehicles, the top priority is to check if there is someone still alive. We go as fast as we can to check for anyone still alive to take them to hospital. Afterwards we remove the bodies. But when we are at the scene of a crime where bullets have been found on the floor, and the cyclist had clearly been killed by bullets, we take extreme caution not to pollute that crime scene. We try to avoid walking over clues, or squashing a cigarette end on which there might be DNA. We didn't open the car doors or anything like that because in doing that we would destroy the clues. The priority with a murder is to find the culprit. If we go too fast we risk destroying clues. I'm sure this would be the same in an investigation in England.

"Our supposition is that the little girl was not asleep but completely terrorised," he continued. "She could feel no one was moving in the car so she curled up into a ball. No one saw her, no one heard her; she made no movements. No one could imagine there was a little girl. Taking all of this into account, I don't think we can have been accused of any errors. What's most important is that she was found alive eventually."

In Britain there was considerable criticism of the decision to wait for the Paris team. It seemed extraordinary. If a murder happens in Leeds, West Yorkshire Police do not wait for a specialist forensic unit to drive up from London before they start examining a crime scene. The gendarmes from Annecy and Chambéry, however, held off on their inquiries until technicians from the Institute for Criminal Research at the Gendarmerie National near Paris had made the journey. It is a fundamental principle of murder investigations that the first few hours after an event has happened are the most crucial. Move incisively and the chances of catching the fleeing assailant are considerably higher. Even if it takes many months or even years to achieve, the evidence collated quickly often turns out to be the most vital in court.

Monsieur Maillaud, however, is adamant it was simply a case of procedure being followed, exactly as would be the case in Britain.

"Ultimately all nations follow the same rules,"

he asserted. "There were laboratories more local than the one in Paris where the technicians came from. We simply made a call to the national laboratory in Paris because we knew we were dealing with something out of the ordinary."

Back then, the day after the killings, Monsieur Maillaud seemed resolutely determined that the perpetrator of this most extraordinary murder would one day be caught.

Speaking many months later, after many long, long days of phone calls and meetings about the case, he was no less dogged.

"In my 25 years as a magistrate I have never had to deal with a crime this terrible," he said. "The most important thing for me is that, many years in the future, I can say to the girls: 'Thanks to the work of the investigators, and their British colleagues, we have found those who killed your parents'."

Meeting Monsieur Maillaud again, he made it absolutely clear he remains true to this vow, even if it takes him through to retirement.

Chapter 5

The aftermath: four burials and two orphaned children

For four awful days Iqbal's sister, Fadwa al-Saffar, waited at Zainab's bedside. The seven-year-old had been put in a medically-induced coma at Grenoble University Hospital's trauma unit. Medics feared her pistol-whipping injuries were so severe she would be left permanently brain-damaged. She had suffered a fractured skull and a bullet in the shoulder. She had reportedly endured multiple facial injuries that caused two subdural haematoma – traumatic injuries to the brain. The orbital bone around one eye was also fractured, meaning she might be left partially blind.

Twelve heavily armed French police stood guard at all times. Two gendarmerie cars were billeted permanently outside. British Embassy officials had been in Grenoble with the girls since the day after the shooting. No one was taking any chances.

PhD student Fadwa was joined by other relatives of Saad and his wife. Having lived and studied in Berkshire near the al-Hillis' family home for many years, Fadwa was the girls' closest relative after their parents. She geared herself up to be the vital familiar face for Zainab if and when she awoke. Family liaison officers from Surrey, experts in helping the victims of violent crime and their relatives, were also on hand.

On Sunday September 9, Zainab regained consciousness. Prosecutor Maillaud described Zainab's survival as a "miracle" but she was heavily sedated. There was no way detectives could hope to talk to her at length yet. It would be a long time before the schoolgirl could be asked to describe the shooter's appearance in the precise terms investigators would need if they were to make progress with the case.

Maillaud had high hopes that Zainab would eventually be able to provide sufficient detail for a precise picture of the assassin to emerge. "We do hope that at seven she is old enough to tell us what she saw," he said at the time. "She can tell us the colour of the skin, the colour of the clothes and other information we need."

As he remarked, Zainab was "the only person alive who actually could have seen something".

Her first words, when they came, were heartbreaking.

"I am so scared. What is happening?" she said, according to one source at the hospital.

The same day little Zeena, her survival a miraculous story of hope amid the savagery of the killings, flew back to London with a British family liaison officer. She had told police as much as she could about the carnage, but even skilled investigators specialised in talking to young children could not prize much detail from her. She could talk in a general, child-like way about her own fear, and she told detectives about the noise as shots were fired, but she knew nothing about her parents' killer's appearance. In Zeena's memory, the attack was a series of terrifying ear-splitting noises and then a veil of silence. Any parent of a four-year-old knows their mind skips so swiftly from moment to moment that although a lot of information is retained it might not come to the surface when grown-ups ask about it.

Zeena journeyed home under conditions of utmost secrecy. To assume the killer had left the area would have been foolhardy in the extreme. Whoever police were dealing with was so callous he would have been quite prepared to add Zeena to his tally of victims to ensure she was unable to provide any useful information.

Zeena was back in the UK in time for the second week of term. That day she should have been getting to know her new classmates and her first form teacher. Instead she was bewildered, traumatised and unable to understand the terrible fate that had befallen her. She would not be going back to Claygate. She would not be able to see her playgroup friends again or playfully run around the family's back garden to the delight of the family's neighbours.

The following day, September 10, Zainab was able to talk briefly to police. As she did, doctors monitored her condition, anxious to make sure the investigators did not push her too far. She was extremely weak, still under sedation, and the gravity of what had taken place was still seeping into her young mind. All she could tell police was that there had been "one bad man".

Then her condition regressed for several days and doctors only gave the green light for her to go home on Thursday of the following week, eight days after she was admitted. Before she left, one more bedside interview took place. It provided some help, saying that she saw a 4x4 vehicle, but nothing emerged that could categorically pinpoint the killer.

Then she returned home to an undisclosed location. Now the investigators had no witnesses left in France.

For Zainab and Zeena, in the care of the British police, safety was paramount. In the short-term they were put under the care of social services.

The authorities were still unpicking the details of the parents' background, trying to establish exactly who was who in the immediate family and if anyone might pose a threat. It was therefore decided the girls would have to stay with an experienced foster family, people who were completely neutral and whose only interest in the girls was providing them with all the help they needed.

The family home on Oaken Lane remained out of bounds. Whatever treasured possessions Zainab and Zeena had there would have to be sent on, like Zainab's fluffy toy penguin. She was so attached to it that caring dad Saad had kept four identical ones, distraught family friends remember.

In France cyclist Sylvain Mollier's memorial service was held on September 17, nearly two weeks after his death. It was several more weeks before his family could have his remains cremated due to lengthy police autopsy examinations. The service in his home town of Ugine was completely private and no one outside his tight-knit circle of friends and family was admitted. The family's wishes for no intrusion at a time of overbearing grief were respected.

A brief obituary published in local newspapers read: "Claire, his love; Leo, Mathis and Louis, his three beloved children; Suzanne, his mother; Alain, Christophe, Francois, his brothers; Sylviane, his sister… his friends, have the sad duty of informing you of the death of Sylvain Mollier, brutally taken on September 5, 2012. You were a father, born in 1967, accomplished amateur sportsman, on paternity leave and working at Ugitech; you had decided to try out a new cycle route passing through Doussard and Chevaline in the Haute-Savoie and you found yourself at the wrong moment in the wrong place."

On Sunday October 21, 2012, seven weeks after their murders, Saad, his wife Iqbal and his mother-in-law Suhaila al-Allaf were buried side by side in the same grave, next to where Saad's parents, Kadhim and Fasiha, were buried in the Shia Muslim section of Brookwood Cemetery near Woking. Zainab and Zeena were not present. Their final resting place was in a quiet corner of what is one of the biggest graveyards in Britain. The site was secluded by pine trees, a pretty spot in the Surrey countryside which Saad had grown to love.

Beforehand, in a traditional ceremony arranged by the Iraqi embassy in London, dozens of mourners attended a special prayer service at the Imam Khoei Islamic Centre in Queen's Park, North West London. Among the pallbearers was Suhaila's brother, and Iqbal's uncle, Dr Ahmad al-Saffar, who had travelled over from his home in Sweden. Saad's close friend James Mathews waited outside as the coffins emerged. In accordance with tradition, the mourners held out their palms while prayers were said. Dr Zaid Alabdi, the family's close friend ever since Iqbal arrived in the UK, was there too. Then, followed by some 30 close relatives, friends and officials, the three plain wooden caskets were driven 40 miles to the cemetery.

Women wailed and men who had earlier tried to restrain their emotions sobbed openly as the coffins were opened, one by one, so the victims' bodies could be faced towards Mecca before they were lowered into the ground.

Incense sticks fizzled and a steady drizzle soaked the huddle of mourners.

The Imam, respected Iraqi scholar Ayatollah Dr Sayyid Al-Milani, led the graveside prayers. In accordance with Muslim custom, the women covered their heads and stood back from the graveside, all the time clutching bouquets which had become soggy in the miserable weather. The men, apparently oblivious to the mud ruining their suits, banded together with their shovels to create a huge, dome-shaped tomb while the steady rain continued to fall. Saad's brother Zaid and the others took up shovels to cover the remains with soil.

All the while, from a discreet distance, Surrey Police detectives observed the scene.

Chapter 6

The evidence

In the days and weeks following the slaughter, detectives in France and Britain undertook painstaking searches at any and every relevant location, looking all the while for the one clue that would unlock the case.

Scores of forensic specialists in white plastic coveralls scoured the inside of the al-Hilli family home on Oaken Lane, Claygate, as well as Saad's self-built sheds and garden storage areas. Given his reputation for keeping everything and creating his own workshop and computer suite at home, this was always going to be a lengthy task. It took weeks. The Monday after the murders an army bomb disposal unit was called to the property after "items of concern" were discovered by officers but they were later ruled non-hazardous. Among many items of interest retrieved from the house was a Taser gun, which would only be explained much later.

As in any case though, the most important site was the murder scene. Here they found no fingerprints, no CCTV of the scene or on the road leading up to it. There were no eye-witnesses other than Zainab, who remained in a serious condition in Grenoble Hospital. The assassin was, according to criminologists looking into the case, "forensically aware" and left no personal property, no clothing, no jewellery which might be taken for a DNA sample.

Police did retrieve two mobile phones from Saad's car. These would contain vital call and text records revealing who he, Iqbal and, perhaps, Suhaila, had been talking to in the days and hours leading up to the murders. There were also tens of thousands of emails to be analysed on Saad's computers in the caravan and at his Claygate home, as well as logs from his chatroom and online Skype messenger exchanges.

Slowly, after a close examination of ballistics evidence, tyre marks in the track and other physical evidence, the investigators began to build up a picture of what had happened.

This much they knew: By 3.40pm on Wednesday

September 5, 2012, a killer using a Swiss Luger P06 7.65mm Parabellum semi-automatic pistol had fired 21 shots: four into Saad, four into Iqbal, three into Suhaila, five into the cyclist Sylvain, one into young Zainab and four into no human target. The dead each had clinical shots to the forehead, Zainab had a wound to her shoulder.

Saad probably took his first shot, to his back, while he was outside the car. Certainly, Saad and Zainab both left the car at the clearing at some point while the other members of the family did not. At least one of the shots to Sylvain was fired before Saad reversed the car across the clearing, and as Saad reversed the killer was firing. Once the car was stationery in the earth bank, the killer carefully and deliberately pulled the trigger for each shot through the side windows. The doors to the maroon BMW were closed and locked when the car was found.

Beyond those very bare facts, the police had nothing but questions.

Was Sylvain shot one more time than the others simply because he was a more difficult moving target? Why did Saad and Zainab get out of the car? Why was Zainab not killed? Did the otherwise merciless killer draw on a shred of humanity and, having maimed and disabled the seven-year-old, decide her life was to be spared? Or did he run out of bullets or his gun jam, so he struck out at the little girl with the butt of his gun to incapacitate or even kill her?

The police did not know. They did not even know which of the 21 shots was fired first.

"We do not know whether the first shot that was fired hit a human target," Monsieur Maillaud said. "Twenty-one were fired and 17 hit a human target. Was it in the direction of Saad al-Hilli at the moment when he said to his daughter: 'Get in the car'? Or was it the cyclist? Zainab says she didn't see a cyclist. Four shots ended up in the forest, but we cannot say if these were fired before bullets hit human targets."

The very lack of evidence and the minimum disturbance to the scene seems pretty certain proof of one thing at least: this was a highly professional killing. The French police described "clinical shots to the centre of the forehead", an act of ruthless precision, as well as "gross savagery", another soundbite given in the police press briefings.

The most revealing analysis was of the gunman's

weapon and the bullet casings. The killer's choice of weapon has remained a topic of much debate.

Monsieur Maillaud explained to me how the detectives are sure the gun was a Luger P06. "Two weapons experts carried out a detailed analysis," he told me. "They found a piece of the covering from the grip of the gun that they were able to take away. A chunk of that handle plaque was discovered on the floor. This was an important clue. On this piece of the handle, we were able to find some blood; it was Zainab's blood we established because it contained her DNA. That's how we can be almost certain a Luger P06 was used, and that the handle was used to crack Zainab's skull."

The Luger is an 80-year-old weapon formerly used by the Swiss army, not as powerful as a modern 9mm pistol but experts say it can be more accurate. Tests reveal it can fire 48 shots in 28 seconds. To choose such a weapon, the gunman was assuming he would be up close to his target. This detail more than any other suggests this was not a random killing. A crazed gunman would have strafed his targets indiscriminately, with many shots missing their targets.

The Luger P06 fires rounds from cartridges

of eight, suggesting the gunman reloaded twice to fire his 21 bullets. That would leave three bullets, implying the weapon had perhaps jammed when the gunman came to Zainab or that he anticipated others arriving at the scene shortly.

But, as with most things in this case, on closer inspection that is not entirely certain.

"We know that the P06 has a magazine containing eight bullets," Monsieur Maillaud clarified. "We know that 21 shots were fired. So, three times eight is 24. Logically, three magazines containing 24 bullets available, but only 21 were fired. This raises questions. According to the experts, there is only one magazine available for this gun. However, we have been told by certain former members of the Swiss armed forces that this gun would deteriorate and the way to prevent that happening was to insert seven bullets instead of eight in the magazine. Now it becomes three times seven: 21. We can imagine the killer fired his last bullet into the shoulder of Zainab, who was still alive. He had no more ammunition, so he pistol-whipped her skull to try to kill her. That is the most likely theory."

Through interviews with arms collectors in the region, the French team has discovered that

P06 pistols can be customised to use a homemade "snail magazine". This is a circular magazine containing many more rounds which transform the pistol into a rudimentary submachine gun able to fire in quicker, more intense volleys, but losing accuracy in the process. Monsieur Maillaud said collectors claim to have seen such customised guns in Switzerland.

"If that were the case, we could have many more than 24 bullets in the magazine, but we have no way of knowing because we don't have the gun," Monsieur Maillaud said.

The Luger P06 was "an intelligent choice" of weapon for someone wanting an "an untraceable gun", a French police source told me. Men who do their military service in Switzerland have historically been allowed to keep their guns when they finish, making this standard-issue pistol so widely owned as to be untraceable.

"In Eastern Europe guns like Kalashnikovs would be equally untraceable, but if someone knew they were doing this around here it is a particularly good choice," the police expert said.

Here is one potential scenario based on the available evidence: Assassin surprises Saad on foot outside his car and shoots him in the body.

Zainab is hidden somewhere at the scene. Saad manages to get into the car and locks the doors. The assassin sees the cyclist Sylvain pedalling towards him and fires twice at him. Saad reverses the vehicle but it gets wedged into the bank as the assassin calmly approaches the side of the vehicle. He shoots Saad again. Mollier is now crawling away from his bike. The assassin shoots him again. He returns to the car and fires at Saad, Suhaila and Iqbal. Reload. He calmly takes careful aim and fires at the heads and necks of the three adults in the car, in Saad and Iqbal's case several times, perhaps because they continued to move until he could be certain they were dead. Reload. He strolls over to the near motionless form of Mollier and shoots him several more times. The final bullet to Mollier's forehead, I can reveal, was at close range, probably while the prone Frenchman was still conscious. The killer sees Zainab at the other end of the parking bay and shoots her once, only managing to hit the shoulder. The pistol jams even though three bullets remain. He strides over to Zainab, hits her hard on the head with the butt of the gun, and then departs by car. He speeds up the hill, not passing Brett Martin a long way further down the otherwise deserted road.

This, of course, is just one possible version among many. The Anglo-French investigating team will probably never be able to precisely clarify the exact order in which the victims were attacked.

One aspect of the evidence is particularly troubling. When Brett Martin got to the scene, the doors of the car were locked. Zainab, however, was found outside the car. The fact Saad and Zainab both left the car was proved by studies of the traces of soil on the soles (of their shoes). Other family members had remained inside the vehicle.

But why? Had Saad reversed the car from its initial position in a panic when the hitman arrived and fired the first shot? Or had he already been shot when both he and Zainab were out of the vehicle? In this second appalling scenario, was he able to jump into his seat, turn on the ignition and haul the car into reverse? Was he forced to make the most awful choice any parent could ever make: flee the scene with one child safely inside and abandon the other, or stay with the girl outside the car in the knowledge that this means the whole family will be slaughtered?

Whatever happened, the car remained jammed in the bank and the killer methodically shot dead his victims. One of the rear tyres was flat and there were a few dents in its otherwise flawless lower bodywork.

Police wasted no time in conducting door-to-door enquiries in Chevaline. As the mayor Didier Berthollet pointed out: "The police interviewed everyone in the village hoping to find a witness. There are only 70 homes, so it didn't take them long."

The vast majority of locals heard nothing, including builder Laurent Fillion-Robin, who saw Saad's maroon BMW pass while he was working on a Chevaline house for British couple John and Vivienne Bewick.

The only people who heard the shots were a 15-year-old boy, identified locally as Melvin Mirabells, who was somewhere up the Combe d'Ire on his scrambler 125cc motorbike, and his father Franck. On hearing the gunfire, Melvin simply continued. He did not bother looking at his watch. Only some time later when he saw fire engines rushing past him to the scene did he realise something bad had occurred. Franck, further down in Chevaline, was surprised only because this was before the start of the hunting season. He assumed some hunters were testing out their rifles and thought little more of it. No one seemed to be able to pinpoint precise timings.

What the detectives did have were a few sightings of vehicles heading away from the Combe d'Ire track and down through Chevaline in the minutes after the murders took place. The most crucial of these sightings came from Brett Martin.

In his interview, Brett admitted he was so tired from "grinding up a steep hill on my mountain bike" that he was less than 100 per cent sure of what he had seen. He was focused on the road in front of him because of the physical exertion required. But he did remember a car, a car that might have been significant.

"I had a recollection at some point of probably a 4x4 coming past me," he was able to recollect later. "It was a large vehicle. And again a motorbike at some point passed me going down… they were the only noticeable things for anybody coming down before I reached the car park."

Detail from this interview enabled something like a timeline to emerge. Brett said the motorbike passed him going down the hill between three and five minutes before he reached the car park cycling uphill. Mollier had overtaken him approximately 25 minutes before reaching the scene. The 4x4 came down the hill past him about halfway through the 25-minute climb. Therefore, if the motorcyclist was the killer, he must have concluded his business by 3.40pm and then sped off back towards Chevaline. If the driver of the 4x4 car was involved, he, she or they, must have left Le Martinet by 3.30pm.

Brett said he did not take notice of the occupants of the car, and he was also unable to describe the motorcycle rider. "I didn't get much detail on the car because I was just riding my bike and they were just some arbitrary cars that were passing me as every car on every day of the week does," he said.

One more chilling fact emerged from Mr Martin's testimony, though. He told police he saw the little girl, Zainab, swaying and then falling. At the moment that Brett arrived, the killer was most likely still incredibly close to the scene, Monsieur Maillaud said to me.

"We have no reason to suspect Mr Martin, but an investigator should always keep an eye on a witness who arrives at the scene of a crime at the precise moment after it has happened," he said. "We have to ask, 'Do we have a witness or do we have something else?' Of course we had to ask that question, but nothing suggested to us that he was anything other than a witness. If he is a genuine witness, as we believe, he must have arrived in the seconds, tens of seconds at the most; definitely not more than a minute after the killer left. That is sure."

Asked if Brett would have seen the killer go past him if he had descended the same route up the Combe d'Ire road, Monsieur Maillaud replied: "Of course, he would have done. So the logic is that he must have gone a different way."

Are they confident, therefore, that the killer instead followed the route over the mountain, the track forbidden for cars? The tarmac surface continues for a further two kilometres, even though it is restricted.

"It is very possible," he responded. "From the parking, the path continues, and then we can go down and rejoin the route on the other side. It's very easy on a motorbike, it's very easy in a 4x4; it is even do-able in a normal vehicle. You would bump around a lot, but if you are not too worried about the condition of your vehicle it's feasible. The police did it in a normal vehicle as part of the investigation. We could also have someone who was on foot."

The day after the attack I interviewed Chevaline resident Sylvie Lecouer who said she had to swerve to avoid a "white Peugeot 306 or 206" coming down the main hill at about 4pm, 15 minutes after the al-Hillis were shot dead.

Madame Lecoeur, then 49, who was driving back from a supermarket, said: "He was coming down the hill on the wrong side. I was terrified. At the last minute he braked and swerved and so did I, so we just avoided hitting each other. It was a small white car, maybe a Peugeot 306 or 206. I think it was a French car, but I can't be sure. There was one man behind the wheel. He was a white man. He had thick, jet black hair, which was cut short. He was wearing a black shirt, a polo neck. He looked very agitated. He was driving as though he was in a car chase. That's why he only saw me at the last second. He gestured with his hands like he was desperate to get me out of the way."

This lead has seemingly not resulted in further police enquiries. It stands alone. No one else seems to have seen the Peugeot.

An avenue that received more scrutiny from the police is Brett's sighting of the 4X4, and the motorbike.

One year after the killings, the testimony of another potentially key witness was made public for the first time. The witness was a forestry worker who was coming down from a nearby mountain above the Le Martinet clearing just minutes before the shooting happened. He spoke to a

Panorama TV documentary crew on condition of anonymity. Here was another person spooked by having an inadvertent cameo in the perfect crime, another innocent person fearful a killer at large might return to Annecy to finish off the witnesses.

"When I arrived there was a motorbike pulling into the parking area," the forestry worker said. "I passed the parking and the motorbike was on the left here. I remember it well. It was white, white and black, with panniers on either side. The rider was all in black; his visor was completely closed."

Crucially, the forestry worker then saw a British-registered 4x4 car on the scene very shortly afterwards.

"He arrived on the left and he passed really quickly," the forestry worker added. "The car was a BMW 4x4, X5, grey metallic, in good condition. It was a right-hand drive, English. I didn't get much of a look at him but the driver was slightly bald and he had dark skin, no glasses."

The 4x4 BMW resulted in an appeal on Crimewatch on the BBC but that provided no more leads. Monsieur Maillaud explained: "The BMW 4x4 was only seen by one person, a forestry worker. Brett Martin didn't see this BMW. He is certain it's a BMW, but he is a bit less certain if it's an X3 or an X5. Everyone thought his testimony was credible. He is someone accustomed to noticing anything out of the ordinary in the forest. A vehicle in a place which is forbidden is something he would remark on. He was also someone quite interested in BMW vehicles. At the same time, investigators are always prudent when there is just a single witness. There was almost certainly a vehicle. For the time being we have not been able to find it."

Approximately ten minutes after this sighting, two of the man's colleagues, also heading down the road towards Chevaline, said they saw the motorbike up from the parking area, at a point where motor vehicles are forbidden.

As we have already seen, the track beyond Le Martinet is intended only for hikers, mountain bikers and the forestry vehicles which need to get higher up for conservation work. It would, as the prosecutor says, be passable by motorbike or a 4x4, but would take about an hour and a half to cover 20 kilometres across the mountain pass. The only permanent resident up there, a shepherd by the name of Denis Janin, saw nothing from his remote chalet.

"They told me they passed the motorbike at Place Martinet, two bends further up," the forestry worker went on. "They had words with him because motor vehicles aren't allowed. So they called out to him and asked him to drive down. They saw his face because he lifted his helmet. He had a bit of a beard."

It seems it was this description which led to the issue of a police artist's impression of a man in a motorcycle helmet in November 2013, a few weeks after the forestry worker's interview was released. The figure in the black and white sketch had a goatee beard, dark eyebrows and an intense gaze. In the description issued with the image, police said the man's helmet was black or dark coloured, chiming with what the forestry workers saw. Tracing the man who matched the e-fit image would provide what, at one point, appeared to be the most significant breakthrough in the case.

However, earlier this year, much to their frustration, detectives finally had to rule out the long-held suspicion that the man on the motorbike was the assassin. He was identified as an "honourable" local man, from Lyon. He was in the Chevaline area "by accident", said the authorities, and they were confident he had nothing to do with the attack. During interviews with detectives, he said he went regularly to the hills above Lake Annecy to practise his passion for paragliding. Monsieur Maillaud said the man was identified and questioned after police cross-checked thousands of telephone records against motorbike licence data. The man, whose identity has been protected, agreed he had been the person driving on the Combe d'Ire road at around 3pm before he was stopped by the two forest rangers. After a fleeting conversation he had agreed to go, he told police. He drove back down the path past the car park. Incredibly, the motorcyclist said he did not "make the connection" between his presence near the scene of the killing and the police picture of him which was circulated in November 2013.

"One of the hypotheses was that the al-Hillis' car was being followed by a motorcycle and a car," Monsieur Maillaud admitted. "It made sense. Now, of course, we have reason to think the motorcyclist was not involved. Before we had a theory with two vehicles, now we have a theory with just one. It becomes a little more complicated."

Police were able to glean some valuable information from the owner of the Solitaire du Lac campsite in Saint Jorioz where the al-Hillis had been staying. This seemingly ruled out the suggestion Saad was at the remote Le Martinet clearing for a specific reason.

"We are virtually certain that the al-Hilli family wanted to go for a walk that day," Monsieur Maillaud told me, revealing this crucial detail for the first time. "We are almost certain too that they ended up there by chance; perhaps by mistake, but in any case by chance.

"The campsite manager told the investigators that Mr al-Hilli, who knew the region and had already been here several times, asked him whether he knew of an agreeable place not too far away to go for a walk. He told them about that general area, but not that exact parking. We think he might have taken the wrong route to end up on the Combe d'Ire road. At the same time it is a start point for a hike because there is the sign there indicating different routes. It is a place frequently used by walkers. We also have the testimony of Zainab who indicated to the investigators that on that day, her dad Saad asked her what she wanted to do. Did she want to do some shopping, to go into town, or did she want to go walking in the mountains? She indicated that she said to her dad, 'I would like to go in the mountains'. In other words, it was Zainab who decided the itinerary for that afternoon. This means the family went there by accident."

Chapter 7

Saad al-Hilli

Saad al-Hilli was born in Baghdad in 1962 to a wealthy Shia family from the city's cultured and highly educated elite. The Iraqi capital was then a pleasant, palm-fringed metropolis bearing little resemblance to the place more recently ripped apart by conflict.

The family name originates from the city of Al-Hillah on the banks of the Euphrates in central Iraq, near the remains the ancient city of Babylon. One of the first al-Hillis was an important Shia scholar in the 13th century although, according to several close friends, Saad, was far from fervent in his religious practice.

Saad's father, Kadhim al-Hilli, was a wealthy businessman whose empire included Iraq's first Kleenex factory, a poultry farm and a works that processed the mineral gypsum. Exactly what caused the family to uproot themselves from their family and friends and leave the country of their birth is not known for certain, but it is most likely the major factor was fear over the security of the business and the family under the new Ba'ath Party government, which was Sunni-led and hostile to Shias like the al-Hillis. It has also been suggested that Kadhim fell out personally with party stooges close to Saddam Hussein – then well on his way to being crowned leader of the Republic in 1979. Perceived enemies of the ruling party were already being singled out by the murderous Mukhabarat secret police.

What is certain is that in 1971 Kadhim, his wife Fasiha and his sons Zaid, then 12, and Saad, then 9, fled to Pimlico, London. Although Kadhim travelled back and forth to Iraq for several years, the family knew there was no going back and they embraced life in their new home. Saad thought of himself as British, as British as his many friends who were born here.

Saad and Zaid were educated at a Pimlico comprehensive and the younger brother easily passed O-levels and A-levels, showing talent in maths, physics and technical drawing. He went on to study engineering at Kingston University, in South

West London. In 1984, when Saad was 22, the al-Hilli family moved to a house on Oaken Lane in the north Surrey village of Claygate. The family liked village life and quickly integrated. They could walk to Claygate's small shopping parade or the station to take a train into London.

They bought the detached property for around £28,000 and it is now estimated to be worth more than £800,000. It would later become Saad and Iqbal's family home… and a source of great rancour between Saad and Zaid.

Earlier, though, this spacious house, with its mock-Tudor rendering on the upper floor, was a hub around which Saad and Zaid would orbit surrounded by their parents' mementoes. They liked the garden, the quiet street and got on well with their neighbours. The boys, especially Saad, loved their doting mother. Their relationship with their father was more complex, with talk that he was a domineering presence and even violent against his wife. Saad was still living there with his mother when she died, when he was 41. Kadhim had by then retired to Malaga, the couple having separated.

After graduating Saad forged himself a career as a mechanical engineer and aeronautics consultant, later specialising in computer-aided design of satellite technology. Kingston, on the edge of London, close to the Surrey countryside, would remain an anchoring point in his life.

Saad was a popular guy with men and women. He was a joker, full of life, and always willing to help others. One man that knew him well back then was Gary Aked, a fellow engineer. They met in bizarre circumstances but became lifelong friends.

"I was dating a girl and we split up," Gary, now 54, told me at his home in Cranleigh. "I discovered she was dating someone else at the same time she was going out with me. She said she's met this chap, but we stayed friends. I got a job soon after for a company called Tanshire Holdings and then, soon after that, the company needed contractors to work in the evening. One evening I met this chap, Saad. He said to me, 'Are you Gary?' I said yes and then he said, 'We've got someone in common.' He then said the name of the girl I'd been dating. I looked at him and said: 'You're the guy who nicked her from me!' And we've been good friends ever since. He went out with her for about six years. It was quite a serious relationship. She bought a house around 1995 just outside Claygate and Saad was doing it up for her. Saad lived with his mum all this time. I remember we would all go for meals together to local restaurants; despite what had happened we all got on well. I think he wanted to get married but he split up with her in the mid to late 1990s."

Saad was a man who could turn his hand to anything. He would not be daunted by any building project in the house or any mechanical failing with his or someone else's car. Rather than hire an expert, he would always have a go at fixing things himself.

"When Saad was doing up that house for his girlfriend I remember thinking how good he was," Gary told me. "Absolutely nothing would faze him. She had a water tank that was rusting so he just took it out and replaced it with a combination boiler which was quite new in those days. I was there once when he was replacing the whole ceiling in the kitchen. Because I was tall and he was quite short, he asked me to hold it up while he was on a ladder nailing it in. He would always say, 'It's easy; I can do this'.

"He was always doing up the parents' house as well. On one occasion I remember he was replacing the heating pipes for the whole house, something I could never imagine doing."

For a lot of his friends a visit to Saad's house would mean lending a hand on some job he was doing, something to which none of them seemed to object.

"Saad always had me doing things because he was always busy," Gary added. "Sometimes I would be mowing the lawn while he was doing something else. He had thousands of projects he wanted to do but there was never enough time for him. I don't know when he slept! He had an old Mercedes in the shed he was going to do up. It was something the Germans would have driven in the war. It took over one of the garages. I don't remember him ever watching telly until he had the kids."

One unplanned visit even ended with Gary halfway up a tree while Saad shouted encouragement from the lawn.

"He had these huge conifers he wanted to chop down. He said they were sucking all the water out of the house and putting it in permanent shade. I looked up and thought there was no way we'd get them down. If they fell they would have gone straight through the fence on the other side of his garden or on the house. He suggested doing them in two halves. He said 'You climb up and I'll get the chainsaw up to you.' I was strapped up to this tree in the middle while Saad had a rope to the top half. I had one hand around a branch to hang on and in the meantime I was trying to cut through this trunk. It was so, so dangerous.

I think we called it a day after we eventually got two of the three trees down. It was an example of how determined Saad was."

Gary Aked has nothing but fond memories of his friend whose wit and good humour were stolen from him so abruptly.

"He was a family man. Before their mother died he helped Zaid do up a flat somewhere in Surbiton. They worked together and did it up because they could see the benefits. They blitzed it. They took all the floors out. There were rotten beams so Saad would cut out all the rotten bits and replace the floors, windows and ceilings. He gutted this place and did it up and I think his brother was living there for a while.

"Saad was a very humorous, very amicable bloke," he reminisced. "He was easy to work with. We got on well, and we were both engineers so we saw eye to eye in loads of designs and projects. He worked in various companies and our paths would cross quite frequently. We always stayed in contact. We used to go cycling together in the woods from Claygate. Our relationship was spasmodic, but we would always see each other. When I got married in 1997, Saad came along."

Despite often being involved in grand multimillion pound engineering projects, Saad's earnings were undoubtedly modest compared to most of his neighbours' in the well-heeled London commuter belt where he lived. Nevertheless, he often tried to get away on holidays with family and friends. On one occasion the young al-Hillis spent a happy few days in Annecy. Saad also went away skiing in Italy with his then girlfriend, a British woman named Sam, and Gary Aked.

France was Saad's favoured destination. Nothing better exemplifies his whimsical eccentricity and love of restoration than his decision to purchase an old ruin in the Gironde region in the late 1990s. On one of his many travels across the Channel, it seems the then bachelor snapped up the derelict barn in the centre of the village of Saint-Macaire on the spur of the moment. Like many of Saad's grand projects the dream of having his own bolt-hole in France was never realised. Locals in the village of just 2,000 people remembered Saad doing some work on the roof and installing electricity, but the house remained uninhabitable. When the engineer and enthusiastic workshop inventor died the property had been on the market for several years, but no one seemed interested in buying it. Villagers in Saint-Macaire had vague memories of Saad pottering about over the course of several visits, but his later marriage to Iqbal and the arrival of their children seemingly put an end to his pipe-dream.

Saad's long-term accountant Julian Steadman, who lives around the corner from the al-Hilli home in Claygate, was also familiar with his client's tendency to get carried away restoring old contraptions and vehicles. They saw each other regularly when self-employed Saad handed in his quarterly VAT returns but their relationship was more as friends than merely professional.

"Saad could turn his hand to anything," he told me. "He took one of my computers away one time to see if he could bring it back to life. He had all sorts of gadgets for things to put inside computers, hosting hard drives, all that sort of stuff. He loved tinkering about with anything mechanical. He rebuilt the caravan, the first caravan he had. It got damaged on the road and he completely rebuilt it. Then he bought the one that he took to France that time. Once he came back with the maroon BMW, which was his pride and joy. He picked it up for next to nothing, and it hadn't got that many miles on it either. It was in very good nick and ideal for towing a caravan, a superb bit of kit. He and I had quite a lot in common when it came to caravans and things. We used to chat quite a lot. He also had an interest in motorbikes like me. He was always having fun."

Gary told me Saad worked for a variety of companies in the Surrey area before getting long-term contract work at Surrey Satellite Technology Limited (SSTL) where he was working when he died. One such firm, Gary recalls, was called Elekta, based in Crawley, which specialises in medical products for radiation procedures in hospitals. Gary remembers how Saad fished out a UNIX computer from a skip when the firm had a clear-out of old equipment. He took it home with him despite not being familiar with its complex language before then.

"Saad learned the language, set it up, and then he had it running in this little back bedroom at his house with all the other computers linked into it," Gary said. "This was in the early days of 3D design. I went there once and he was designing something on one computer, looking up something else on another computer, and there were a couple of laptops linked in at the same time on which he was chatting on chatrooms in Arabic. He was into Skype very early on."

Neighbour Jack Saltman, whose garden backs on to the al-Hilli Claygate property, has fond memories of chatting to Saad over the fence. Jack, a retired editor for Thames TV documentary series This Week, met his Iraqi-born neighbour soon after moving in to his detached bungalow in a side road off Oaken Lane. He got on well with all of the family, but Saad in particular made an instant positive impression.

"Soon after I moved in here I saw this chap on the other side of the fence," Jack recalled. "I was trying to clear some ground at the bottom of the garden right next to his fence. I put my spade in and found a concrete path had been laid there, which was now covered in an inch of soil. This chap came over and said, 'You look like you've got a problem.' When I explained, he said, 'Oh, what you need is a mattock.' I didn't know what a mattock was. He went into his shed, in which he had every tool known to mankind, and came out with this pickaxe with a flat blade at one end. He said, 'You'll kill yourself if you do. I'll do it.' So he broke up the path, lifted all the bits of concrete on to his side. He put all of the waste into a skip which he had outside his house. Saad introduced himself by saying, 'My name's Saad, like the Swedish car Saab but with a D.' I remember that well. He was a very happy person."

Skype and the growth of online communication and social networks were to have a profound effect on the way Saad interacted with the outside world. He remained a gregarious, well-liked friend and colleague to many people in Surrey though. And he was devoted to his family, his mum in particular.

Dr Zaid Alabdi, who would later become one of Saad and Iqbal's closest friends in Britain, believes Saad's relationship with his mum Fasiha was the most profound one in his life. He had plenty of girlfriends, but seemingly could not settle down permanently with any of them. Although totally integrated into British life, it is possible Fasiha might have wanted Saad, the youngest of her sons, to marry an Arabic girl. Her views perhaps remained more traditional.

So Fasiha's death in April 2003 had a profound effect on Saad. Those who knew him said he was always closer to her than his father. At the age of 41 he was still living at home with her. They shared a bond that extended beyond childhood. Stricken by grief, he gave up working in Surrey and went to the Middle East.

Dr Alabdi, who runs a dental practice in Kingston, realised that any mention of Fasiha to Saad during conversation would provoke an emotional response. "He had a very exceptional relationship with his mother," he told me when I saw him in February this year. "He really loved her. Every time you mentioned her name he would start crying. The mother had not had a good relationship with his father. I think the father was a bit violent so he was always on her side, and spoke without respect about his dad because of the hurt he caused her.

"He was really close to his mum," Gary too remembers. "When she died he just went; he was very sad and upset. He left the country. The next thing I knew was when he was back in England and he rang me to say, 'I want you to come over and meet my wife.'"

Chapter 8

Iqbal al-Hilli

If Saad and Iqbal were complete strangers before they met in Abu Dhabi in the early summer of 2003, then was Saad a very fast mover? To his friends back in Britain who knew nothing beforehand, it must have seemed as though Saad had worked his magic and charmed the raven-haired 38-year-old in the United Arab Emirates capital.

But I have been told by those who knew Baghdad-born Iqbal in the preceding years, however, that this marriage was effectively arranged by their respective Iraqi families in keeping with their longstanding traditions.

Saad was in Claygate, laying his beloved mother to rest at Brookwood Cemetery in Surrey in May of that year. On August 28, exactly four months to the day after his mum's death, he and Iqbal were getting married at Weybridge register office, an Edwardian manor house.

The wedding was a quiet affair, very traditional. Saad kept it quiet from Gary, one of his closest confidantes, until after it had taken place. The witnesses were Abdul Amir al-Saffar, Iqbal's father, who lived in Sweden with her mother Suhaila, and Zaid, Saad's brother, with whom he was still extremely close. Suhaila, Iqbal's paternal uncle Ahmad, and Saad's father Kadhim are also thought to have been there at the short ceremony.

It seems clear that Saad and highly qualified dentist Iqbal did not meet spontaneously in Abu Dhabi. Several of Saad's friends have told me he wanted to get married as quickly as possible after his mum died to someone of whom she would have approved, an Iraqi and a Muslim. The wedding was thus arranged between the two families, it is reasonable to assume.

"Saad once told me he had married Iqbal to keep his mother happy," his close pal James Mathews informed me. "It was as though he was marrying her in memory of his mum. He didn't have to marry an Iraqi but he had told me a few times that his mother had disapproved of his brother marrying a white European woman."

Gary Aked was stunned by what seemed to be a

shotgun wedding. He believed Saad wanted children more than anything, and he wanted them quickly.

"I couldn't believe it," Gary told me. "I met Iqbal then, when Saad called me some time after their wedding. Saad desperately wanted children. He really loved kids. That was his goal, his aim, everything he had been working for. When I took girlfriends over who had kids, he would be more interested in talking to the kids than anyone else."

The suddenness of the marriage adds to the mystery of an outwardly lovely and gentle couple of whom everyone in their social circle speaks highly. In my research for this book, I have not found anyone even remotely critical of either Saad or Iqbal. They charmed everyone they met. But there is another even odder background fact to the Weybridge wedding.

Iqbal, it has emerged, lied about her marital status on the marriage certificate. On it she refers to herself as a spinster. In fact, she had already been married. Worse still, she was still married to her first husband at the time of the Weybridge ceremony.

Iqbal's still-legal marriage had been in the United States, to a white Harley Davidson biker from Mississippi named James "Jimmy" Thompson, who lived with her in New Orleans. Their relationship ended amicably, by mutual consent, just over two years previously. When she lived in the States she was thoroughly westernised and was known not by her Arabic name, but as Kelly. At weekends Jimmy took Kelly for trips to the beach.

When Iqbal tied the knot to Saad, she was still Mrs Thompson. Six days after the Surrey register office ceremony, she was back in Abu Dhabi, apparently to sign divorce papers. But it was a further two months before the documents came through. This was not only an affront to her new spouse; it was also in breach of marriage law. It was bigamy.

Did Saad know all this, or did Iqbal keep it from him, and tell him she had to go back to Abu Dhabi for an entirely different reason?

And does Iqbal, presumed for so long to be a minor character in this drama, suddenly become a person of interest in the investigation?

The existence of Jimmy the secret husband was revealed last year by French police. They had known about him beforehand, but they kept it quiet from the media. They had, however, been in contact with the FBI, who contacted Jimmy's sister Judy Weatherly in 2013. Until that point, Judy, one of Iqbal's closest confidantes in the US, was still in the dark about the Chevaline murders. The crime was not a big story in Louisiana and Mississippi.

It seems that very few people in Saad al-Hilli's circle knew about Iqbal's previous marriage to Jimmy either. Dr Zaid Alabdi, the al-Hillis' close friend in Kingston, told me he was at first disbelieving when he read news reports about Iqbal being married before. She had never said anything about it to him. But marriage certificates have subsequently disproved everyone's initial doubts: Iqbal was indeed married to former cop and oil worker Jimmy. The ceremony took place in the parish of Jefferson, Louisiana at 1.15pm on July 28, 1999 and was overseen by Justice of the Peace Vernon J. Wilty III.

On the day, portly Jimmy, with receding grey hair and moustache, wore a short-sleeved white shirt and a garishly patterned tie. Iqbal, 20 years younger than her betrothed, had her hair done; long, wavy locks over the shoulders of a figure-hugging sleeveless navy blue dress with an interlocking white leaf pattern. In pictures taken on the day the smiles on their faces do not look strained. Jimmy and Iqbal look happy.

Jimmy and 'Kelly' Thompson lived together in a single-storey suburban bungalow with a large lawn and driveway in a New Orleans suburb called

Marrero, between the Mississippi River and Lake Salvador. A place of sprinklers and long evenings out on the veranda, it was a laid-back location of which someone from a troubled country like Iraq might have dreamed. Iqbal relished her lifestyle in the sunshine, a lifestyle she seemingly had not wanted to give up.

It was her mother, Suhaila al-Allaf – who died at her side in the back of the BMW in France years later – who pressured her to leave the United States, I have been told.

Sabah Alshaikhly, a US citizen of Iraqi origin, had introduced Iqbal to Jimmy. Iqbal - already by then Kelly – lived with Mr Alshaikhly and his then wife in Atlanta, Georgia, for three months just before her marriage. Mr Alshaikhly, 62, who left Baghdad in 1976 says he met Iqbal in early 1999, shortly after she arrived in the US. She was then 34. A doctor friend from Dubai contacted him to say she was looking for a place to stay.

Mr Alshaikhly was an integral part of an extended network of expat Iraqis and at the time he was married to Jimmy's niece.

He felt sorry for Iqbal and helped her by taking her to a nearby university so she could research the qualifications she would need to work as a dentist in the US. But despite her qualifications at home, she was never able to get a job befitting her skill level.

"My friend called me and said Kelly had been in America for a few months and she had no money and nowhere to stay," he explained to a British newspaper last year. "I wanted to be a good person so I let her stay with me in Atlanta. She had moved out here to be a doctor, so I took her to Emory University to see if it was possible. She was already highly qualified, but they said she needed to go to medical school for one year and then take exams. She did not want to do that."

Why then did Iqbal go to the States in the first place? She could not have predicted her marriage to Jimmy Thompson. This is another aspect of the al-Hilli family's complicated history that is difficult to understand.

It was Mr Alshaikhly who introduced Iqbal to Jimmy during a trip to his mother-in-law in New Orleans, Judy Weatherly, Jimmy's sister.

"One day I went to visit my wife's mother in New Orleans and I took Kelly with me," he recalled. "Jim was there and they got on well. We went back to Atlanta, there was contact between her and Jim and then she moved up to live with him. The next thing I heard they had got married. I was happy;

they are both adults so they can do what they want."

Perhaps, having failed to receive permission to work as a dentist, Iqbal was happy to rely on someone else. This still doesn't explain why she would abandon what was by all accounts a good career in Abu Dhabi and go to a country where she hardly knew anyone. Something must have prompted her.

Judy was extremely close to Iqbal during her time in the US. Asked to describe the family's relationship with Iqbal, she told me: "She was with us all the time. We would be at barbecues, my older brother, her and me sitting on a bench. In New Orleans we are always out by the pool; she would be with us playing by the pool all the time."

"We were very, very close," Judy added. "I loved her. I adored her. She was very, very intelligent; I loved that about her. She was very sweet, sensitive; very thoughtful. I saw her every day. If she didn't come over then I'd go over there. She was younger than me but we were very close. She was just a very sweet person."

Describing how Iqbal helped the family out when they needed dental work doing but couldn't afford the bills, Judy added: "My older brother had never had a cavity, but because of his medication his teeth all wore down. She made him false teeth that looked just like his other teeth. She was good at what she did and she was a wonderful person."

She worked four days a week as a dental assistant and was otherwise always going for outings with Jimmy.

"She would cry because people would be rude to her. The people she worked with were ugly to her. She would come to the house sometimes and cry about it. I'd tell her they should know better; you need to find somebody else to work for. She worked part-time so that she and Jim could go and do things more."

Unlike the stay-at-home mum Iqbal of the Surrey years, Kelly was vigorously athletic in the States, Judy said. She was obsessed with her fitness and often spent her spare time running.

"She was slim, she was well-dressed; she wore make-up and her hair down," Judy said. "The

pictures I have seen of her there, she wore no make-up; she was horribly dressed.

I mean, she looked like a pauper. She gained weight. She just let herself go; that just wasn't her. I could tell she was very, very unhappy. It's just two different people as far as I'm concerned."

In September, two months after the marriage ceremony, Iqbal received a letter confirming her permanent resident status in the US. It was addressed to her married name, Iqbal Thompson. In the letter, the Texas branch of the Immigration and Naturalization Service explains that the Green Card will arrive in the post soon. If this was Iqbal's aim, she had achieved it quickly.

Mr Alshaikhly has repeatedly denied that he arranged the marriage to Jimmy so Iqbal could get a Green Card. Yet Jimmy's daughter, Joy Martinloch, disagreed. She claimed Iqbal and Jimmy struck a deal in which the Iraqi woman agreed to buy her potential husband a car in exchange for a sham marriage. Other unnamed family friends last year told journalists the two slept in separate bedrooms and the marriage was purely one of convenience.

Judy insisted otherwise, telling me that her brother and Iqbal lived "as man and wife".

Describing Iqbal days after the Jimmy Thompson marriage was revealed, Mr Alshaikhly said: "I lived with Kelly for a few months and she was super nice, very respectful and very respectable. We went to the mall together and cooked together in the house and she never said or did anything that made me suspect anything was wrong with her. She told me about her family in Iraq and as far as I know there were no political links. We all loved and respected her … We left on good terms and there was no bad blood. Jim loved her. She was happy, but I guess she got homesick. She wanted to leave so he let her leave."

In photographs of Iqbal and Jimmy, she looks like she is having fun. One shows her feeding her husband in the kitchen of their New Orleans home. Another shows them frolicking by the pool, with Jim in his shorts about to hurl his fully clothed wife into the water. In one tender snap he is kissing her on the neck, and she is giggling while being photographed. She looks equally happy sitting on a swing bench in the garden with Judy and her father; or outdoors at a family barbecue on a balmy evening.

If we assume Iqbal went to the United States to get a Green Card, she achieved it by marrying Jimmy Thompson. But after a relatively short time she decided to leave the country, returning to Abu Dhabi less than a year after the ceremony. A fax receipt I have been sent, which was dispatched from the States to Iqbal, puts her back in the Middle East by May 2000. There is also a UAE visa in her passport granted at the same time. Perhaps she was travelling back and forth.

There is another intriguing stamp in Iqbal's

passport from that era. Dated 29/11/00, it says: "UK Los Angeles". The word "withdrawn" is written by hand.

Iqbal might well have decided America was not for her; perhaps she yearned to be back in the Arabic-speaking world. If so, why would she agree to go to England with a virtual stranger to live in suburban Surrey, a setting just as alien to her as Louisiana? On her return to Abu Dhabi she got a good job. From January 2001 until at least April 2003, when Saad arrived, she was a General Practitioner in the Faculty of Dentistry at Ajman University of Science and Technology.

From Marrero, Louisiana, to Abu Dhabi to Claygate, Surrey, in the space of a few years: Iqbal was certainly seeing contrasting parts of the world.

Jimmy's family in the US believe the main reason Iqbal fled her happy life with them in the Deep South was because her own family made her go. They contend that the marriage to Saad was arranged.

Asked her opinion about why Iqbal left New Orleans for Abu Dhabi, Judy replied: "Her mother kept telling her that she needs to marry in her faith and she told her mother she was happy. There was some reason her mother couldn't come here. I really didn't go into it because I didn't ever suspect anything like this going on like it did. I didn't quiz her on it that much. I'm not even certain her mother knew about Jim. She told me a couple of times that she had told relatives that she was just staying with friends and she was having a hard time.

"About two weeks before she left, she said, 'Judy, I'm going to have to go'. She kept blowing it off. I said, 'Kelly, what are you talking about?' I didn't listen to her and then one day Jim told me: Kelly really needs to go. I said, 'Why? Have you done something? Did she do something?' She just told me that she really needs to go. I said I don't understand it because she was my friend. Jim said, 'She's not happy because she's only working as a helper in a dentist's office.' They wouldn't let her be a hygienist; they would just let her be an assistant. She couldn't get her licence. He said that she was unhappy, and that her family was putting a lot of pressure on her to get back.

"I said, 'Are you going back to the Emirates?' because that was where she was living when she came here. She said, 'I'm going to start out over there'. She said her mother was in France at the time. She was going to find her mother or something. I just didn't want her to go.

"She really didn't want to leave, but it was a forced type thing from her family. They just constantly were in contact with her; I guess you'd say bothering her. They were making her feel guilty for being out of her faith, that kind of thing. I'm sure they picked al-Hilli for her. I'm not certain how that came down. When she left we just held each other crying. We walked all the way to the car crying; we were holding each other. The day she was leaving Jim didn't even come over because he said, 'You need your time together'. He was taking her to the airport. It was just a really, really sad day."

So what else do we know about Iqbal, an Iraqi dentist living in Surrey who kept herself to herself, maintained a low profile, but apparently guarded a secret to her entire social circle in Britain and lied about her "spinster" status? Friends are in no doubt Saad would have regarded this lie as a total breach of the absolute trust he had placed in her.

Iqbal was born in Iraq in 1965, the daughter of Abdul Amir al-Saffar and Suhaila al-Allaf. She was an extremely bright girl who did well at school and gained a place at Baghdad University to study dentistry. Little is known about her as a young woman, from her mid-20s to her mid-30s. One man who studied at the university at the same time was Dr Zaid Alabdi, who later became one of the family's closest friends in Britain.

"I was at university in Baghdad with Iqbal from 1982 to 1987," said Dr Alabdi, who runs the Cross Deep Dental Practice in Twickenham, South West London. "During that period I only knew of her, but I didn't really have any direct contact with her. She was a very quiet person. I never heard anything about her, either good or bad. She was always isolated with a couple of close friends."

Dr Alabdi has given me a student line-up photograph from that time, in which Iqbal is stood on the back row. She was around 20 years old at the time. She is a stylish, pretty young woman in a white dress with a beaming smile. Like all of the other female students, her dress is Western.

After that time there is a gap of at least 10 years before Iqbal showed up in the United States. For some of the time before then she was living in the United Arab Emirates. Some evidence, including a stamp in her passport, suggests she was living in America, or at least passing through, as early as 1995. This contradicts Mr Alshaikhly's view she had just arrived when she came to stay with him in Atlanta.

The next time Dr Alabdi thought anything about his Baghdad contemporary was shortly after she had come to England with Saad, her new husband. Unsurprisingly, as most people would expect, he had forgotten about her.

"Saad introduced himself to me one day while I was out shopping," Dr Alabdi recalled. It was a very bizarre opening gambit, but Saad was always refreshingly direct. "He said his wife was at university with me. I said I was sorry but I couldn't remember her; it was a very long time ago. He asked if I would mind if he took my contact. She had just moved to London from Abu Dhabi. He said it would be nice if I could give him some introduction into dentistry here."

Over the following nine years, Saad and Iqbal would become firm friends of the Alabdi family. Dr Alabdi and his wife, who live in a large detached house in Kingston, were more firmly established in their community but did their utmost to make Saad and Iqbal feel welcome. Dr Alabdi also did his utmost to further Iqbal's dentistry career, but she seemed reluctant to make inroads herself despite Saad's efforts on her behalf.

"We used to see them once every two or three months," Dr Alabdi recalled. "We used to call each other about once a month. I used to help him financially because of debts. Sometimes he didn't have enough cash to run his life. I used to ask him to fix the computers at work or install a wardrobe at home, these kinds of things. I used to hand him a few hundred pounds here and there. It was indirect and he knew I was doing it to help him. Every time he used to give me a big hug. He was always troubled for money. He was not a posh person in any way. He didn't wear expensive clothes. His house looks okay from the outside but once you go in it looks very old; it was packed with old stuff.

"We really liked them. We used to feel sorry for them. We have loads of friends and we're a big family. We go out all the time. They don't know anyone. They did not have loads of friends or visitors, so I always tried to get them involved when we had a child's birthday or something like that. We invited them to change their surroundings. If not they just stayed at home. We used to invite them for the children's birthdays. We invited them on Christmas Day too. My parents liked them too. They were easy-going company."

Saad's Claygate next-door neighbour Brian Howells also found the al-Hillis to be a quiet, withdrawn couple.

"Even though they lived next-door we never got to know them particularly well," he told me. "They kept themselves to themselves. They were very private. I chatted with Saad; he was always friendly. He would do anything to help. If my car wouldn't start he'd be round in no time at all. You couldn't have asked for a better neighbour to be honest. Iqbal was much more reserved."

The descriptions of Iqbal could not be more different. In the United States she was larking about by the swimming pool with her playful husband; in Claygate she rarely seemed to get involved in conversations.

Dr Alabdi said: "Of course she never mentioned she was married before," he confirmed. "For an Iraqi woman to say they were married before is like a shameful thing. It would surprise me if Saad knew. Something for sure is that her marriage there was for a Green Card or visa. People from that region are desperate to get out of that region. For a quiet lady to get married to someone she doesn't know and to actually go to the States is extraordinary. Her family are a very strict family. They wouldn't let a girl go on her own to Abu Dhabi, let alone America. They are a very secret family."

Dr Alabdi believes it was only because Saad was

feeling the strain that Iqbal eventually agreed to start training for her British dentistry exams. She passed the first part of the examination and was studying for the second part when she died. She had been a stay-at-home mum since Zainab was born and might perhaps have been rusty. As ever, Saad did his best to help.

"She feared driving, she didn't go shopping, she didn't take the kids to nursery because she was so terrified someone might speak to her, and she never studied for the dental exams at first," Dr Alabdi recalled. "It applied loads of pressure on him, so eventually he told her she would have to start studying. That's why he built the wooden house in the back garden. He bought her equipment to do this. In the last few years of her life she was studying really, really hard."

It was neighbour Jack Saltman who assisted Iqbal in eventually gaining a training placement at Hare Lane Dental Practice in Claygate, a few minutes walk from the al-Hilli home.

"I remember Saad put in electricity in the summer house so his wife could do her dental training in there," Mr Saltman recollected. "I had a word with the man who was my local dentist and he agreed to mentor Saad's wife. Iqbal was a delightful woman.

She was very bright and very sharp. She would have made a very good dentist here. She had already passed Part One of her exams."

"Iqbal remained a very quiet person when we met her during that period of time," Dr Alabdi continued. "She would sit in a chair while we were chatting in my front room and she would smile. If someone asked her something, she answered. If we had a discussion she was not involved. To my knowledge she didn't have friends or go out. After a few years Saad started to get a bit angry with her because she didn't really do anything. Saad was definitely the dominant person in their relationship. He was a very genuine person and I liked him for that. He was a very honourable person. We had a good friendship as families. They used to come and visit us after our eldest girl was born. At the time he was very desperate to have a girl himself. I think they were trying for a child. Eventually they had one."

Chapter 9

Zeena and Zainab al-Hilli

Zainab Saad al-Hilli was born on March 16, 2005, at Kingston Hospital. It was unusually warm for the time of year, a gorgeous spring day. I know this because my own son was born that day. Saad was elated. Aged 43, he had finally achieved his ambition of becoming a father. In accordance with Iraqi tradition Zainab took his name for her middle name.

Gary Aked vividly recalls the change in his friend. "When Iqbal got pregnant he was over the moon," he said.

The change in the family also brought new friends. Soon Saad and Iqbal met James Mathews. His daughter Zorah went to the playgroup at Claygate parish church with Zainab, and the girls' mothers bonded. Iqbal, still a relative newcomer to Britain, had instinctively felt empathy with the only other foreign mum in the room, James' Italian wife Gabriella. Zainab got on well with Zorah and when the two women got chatting about their partners, both knew straight away the men would get on too.

James, who is now 56, was of a similar age to Saad and by his own admission also "a bit of a geek". The pair connected straight away. That was in 2006, and over the following years James and Saad would be in constant contact.

"We met through our daughters' playgroup in 2006," James, who now lives in a flat in Kingston, told me. "Zainab was about a year old and my daughter had not been born that long. My wife was Italian and Claygate is a small town, so my wife made a bee-line for the outsider because she feels a bit of an outsider herself. Iqbal was an intelligent, slightly older mother, which is how my wife thought of herself. They were both outsiders in a small village. After they had become friends I was invited around to meet Saad because it was obvious we would both get on. We were both geeks. Saad had a garage full of all sorts of crap: computers, bicycles, bits of machinery. He was a bit of a hoarder. I would like to be a hoarder but I didn't have much space. We used to swap things. In fact, I've still got one of his printers. He would collect old bits of computers and then rebuild them. The garden shed, which he built by himself with the help of various tall friends when he couldn't reach, was a workroom. It had four workstations and it had a server."

To James, Zainab's natural intelligence shone out.

"Zainab was very, very bright," James reflected during our interview. "If Zainab asked 'why?', like lots of children do, you would have to give her chapter and verse. You couldn't just answer, 'because the sky is blue'; you would have to explain the reasons for the sky's composition! She was so bright that she thought I was immature! She thought that when me and her dad got together we should behave in a much more adult way. She thought adults should be much more adult.

"She was always very interested in flowers. I also remember that she had a very high reading age. She was extremely inquisitive, and what really made her stand out was that she was incredibly polite. She was very much a daddy's girl, always hugging and kissing daddy.

"She thought in English and spoke in Arabic when necessary. She would use Arabic because she knew that was her historical, genetic language. But she always thought in English. She'd use English grammar and a few Arabic words."

Three years after Zainab, on April 24, 2008, Zeena was born, again at Kingston Hospital. The age gap was similar to the one between Saad and his brother Zaid. It was not an easy birth, and with Iqbal now 43, it appeared the couple had missed their chance to have a son, but that did not seem to bother either of them in the slightest.

"Zeena was a very difficult pregnancy for Iqbal," James informed me. "Later Zainab would always look after her sister and be the big sister towards her. As she grew up Zeena became incredibly tactile. She was much more cuddly, more childish and more trusting than her big sister. She was very funny. She was always looking for attention; she would perform. If she thought there was a smile in it she would do something funny. They were quite different characters."

Dr Zaid Alabdi remembers both al-Hilli girls as being reserved: "My children are older than theirs. Zainab is slightly younger than my youngest, my son. My kids are very outspoken but if you spoke to Saad's kids you would hardly get a reply from them. They would hide behind their mum and dad. When they came here they would follow their mum around."

Saad was at his happiest when playing with his daughters, revelling in the chance to bring his carefree side to the fore. Jack Saltman saw his neighbour having fun with his daughters over the fence that separated their two gardens.

"Saad adored those little girls," he said. "He absolutely worshipped them. If I was talking to the girls by my fence and he came into the back garden he would come over and smother them in kisses. He was a very cuddly father.

"I also used to chat with the girls quite a lot," he continued. "Zainab was very articulate, quite a serious young girl. Her little sister was a very bubbly little thing. Being a little bit hard of hearing, half the time I couldn't understand what she was saying and I had to get Zainab to translate for me. They were permanently together. They played all the time. I remember we bought Easter eggs one year and gave them to the girls over the fence."

Saad's accountant Julian Steadman would see his friend and client dropping Zainab off at Claygate Primary from his home office nearby. "He loved those kids; he absolutely adored them," Mr Steadman told me. "He used to cycle down my road to drop them off at school. I used to see him a lot."

Gary Aked's impressions were just as strong: "He loved those two girls so much. When they came home he would grab them and hug them. He was so tactile. He said to me once that he wanted to earn as much money as he could for the girls to be secure; he wanted the girls to have a future. He wanted them to be happy and well schooled. He wanted them to have a good life. In some ways I think his wife was there to produce the kids. He and Iqbal were close, but not as close as other people I know."

What gave Saad most joy away from the stresses of work and paying the bills was packing up the whole family and going away. The caravan was always parked on the front driveway, its bracket facing the right way to be clipped on to the car on a whim.

"They would take the caravan six miles down the road and go camping at the Caravan Club in West Horsley," James said. "Often he just wanted to get away from home, to go somewhere with very little mobile phone signal."

"He loved driving," Gary Aked said. "He'd just stick the caravan on the back of the BMW and go off. He was very independent."

In 2011, the year before the murders, Saad

packed the maroon BMW, fitted the roof rack for the bikes and clipped on the caravan for a week's holiday in France.

Saad took hundreds of photographs on that camping trip. A handful have been made public, but close friends and former colleagues have been told not to release any more by the police. For this book I was allowed access to many of them.

At the time the pictures were taken, Zeena was only three and Zainab was six. The album begins with Zeena and Zainab eating a snack on the cross-Channel ferry. After arriving at a Les Castels campsite, they explore their new surroundings: they play on a climbing frame, Zainab on a yellow slide and Zeena on a tyre swing. Leaning over a bridge that crosses a small brook with their mum they point to the water, perhaps looking for ducks and fish. They draw at the table in the caravan, which they called "Spotty" because of its slightly garish décor. Later in the day, the pair lie back together, Zeena leaning on Zainab, to watch a DVD on their father's laptop.

A strict court injunction prevents me from describing the girls' features, their hair, the colour of their eyes or their complexion. Both daughters are always colourfully and unpretentiously dressed. They and their mum wear plastic Croc sandals or Wellington boots. The youngsters wear flowery sleeveless dresses over mismatched tops and leggings. Zeena always seems to be in the same outfit, a yellow dress with pink trim, pink leggings and blue plastic boots. Zainab wears a pink Puffa jacket.

On the pictures go. Zainab and Zeena hold green clothes pegs in front of their eyes, a silly, childish moment captured for posterity.

Dozens show Zainab pedalling around the site on one of Saad's many creations: the back part of a tricycle fitted with two plastic seats at the rear, a bracket for either a child's bike or the tandem for him and Iqbal at the front.

Then the girls try out toy bikes on a soft playground surface at the campsite, pushed around by a shyly smiling Iqbal, wearing a green fleece jacket and black trousers.

At the campsite's bouncy castle Iqbal sits on the edge while the girls jump around behind her with another child. Then Iqbal must take the camera because Saad is there, jumping on to the bouncy castle and cuddling Zeena.

In yet another picture, Zainab has a front tooth missing. How many more lost teeth, how many other little milestones in the girls' lives have their parents missed since?

Those smiles. Zainab and Zeena are always smiling. They are cute, pretty, adorable. Zainab is usually taking care of her little sister, guiding her, holding her hand, showing her something or talking to her.

The final shots show the family out on a cycle ride together. Zainab and Zeena off the bike to feed grass to some goats at a farm.

Two girls revelling in nature. Lively, curious and secure under the gaze of their loving parents.

Less than eighteen months later, they would be orphans.

Chapter 10

Scared for their own lives: the al-Hillis leave Claygate

Saad al-Hilli: Claygate Mr Fixit, charming practical joker with a winning smile, respected design engineer with a wealth of experience, doting dad, sensitive husband and caravanning enthusiast.

All these characterisations of Saad are true; however from my extensive conversations with several of those who knew him best it becomes apparent he was also a very troubled man in the year before his death. Indeed, an analysis of his state of mind in the lead-up to his fatal trip to France reveals a far more complex picture. It is a picture of a man troubled by money worries – worries entangled with the death of his father and the breaking down into acrimony of one of the most important relationships of his life. Saad had his cheery public persona, but sometimes his mask slipped.

Some of the most revealing insights into Saad's character come through the lighter side of his often frenetic online chats with his friends.

James Mathews has given me a full transcript of the Skype Messenger exchanges with Saad over a two-year period from 2010 to 2012. Many of the comments in it between Saad and James are simple quips and banter. They are happy to send messages back and forth about their journey home, how many hours they have worked, why they were woken up early and other practical details about car fuel and mileage. They jokingly call each other "darling" and "sweetie". The men chat, back and forth, about wintry weather, about ice on the roads, about making dinner and about police cars getting stuck trying to climb up a hill because they don't have proper traction for the heavy vehicles.

The message log begins in November 2010. Saad makes a reference to Iqbal's sister being over to stay and her having to go to Gatwick early to take a connecting flight back to Iraq. This is probably a reference to Fadwa al-Saffar, now the girls' principal guardian in Britain.

On December 14, 2010, Saad says "missing my Zeena" while he is working at the SSTL office in Guildford. He then sends a message with a sad face symbol, but goes on: "I had a good long cuddle though this morning". He also tells James he is waiting for the delivery of a tow-bar for his BMW, presumably the same tow-bar used to take the caravan to France. What shines through these messages is Saad's slightly geeky passion for his car and his very strong affection for his family.

The conversation goes on for several pages on the subject of James' own domestic life – the men are well acquainted with each other's domestic tribulations.

On some occasions Saad asks his best mate a DIY-related question out of the blue. For example, he asks the cost of hardcore, joking that he means rubble for a new driveway rather than "blue stuff". Saad seems to be well-versed in trade websites, knowing the best places to buy and sell second-hand materials for his many projects. He ends one chat by telling his friend he has a buyer coming over to pick up a wheelchair lift he had bought in Birmingham. He is continually involved in money-making schemes of one kind or another.

Saad seems to have his computer switched on 24 hours a day, and was frequently awake in the early hours. On December 16, at 2.48am, James logs on and Saad sends him a message saying: "and what time do you call this!!!" Their messages carry on either side of the Christmas period. Often Saad is the reassuring voice.

Imagining him typing away furiously at 3am while his wife and children are asleep conjures an image of someone not entirely content. As the parent of a toddler, surely a happy Saad would have been conserving his energy for the morning.

He contacts James after 2 in the morning on January 1, 2012, after finishing New Year's Eve celebrations with Iqbal. Asked by James what he was doing at midnight, he says: "I was with Zainab as she could not get to sleep …we were up till 1am". He adds later "if you force her she will get upset and it all gets worse". The tight bond between father and child is obvious.

The online conversation moves on to the topic of teenagers and 20-somethings going to illegal raves on New Year's Eve. Saad, ever protective, types: "I would not even let my girls out of the house if there is crap like that around."

He displays much affection towards Zeena too, talking of how he is sitting down to watch a Tom and Jerry cartoon with her one day. In another exchange he tells James he is wrapping up her presents. Saad was obviously a hands-on dad. He is the one taking Zainab to Kingston to look for her first classical guitar, an event he refers to in one entry.

In January 2011 the log features its first reference to his brother Zaid, with whom he is still on very good terms. Saad asks James if he can drop him off at St George's Hospital in Tooting, South London, for a minor sinus operation. He comments that his brother will be able to collect him later to save his friend hanging around for hours. By the end of the year, as we shall see, it will be a very different picture.

That same month Saad declines an invitation to go to a 50th birthday party with James, explaining that Iqbal is studying on a mannequin dummy in the office all weekend, presumably in preparation for her British dentistry exams. Later that same day Saad confirms he is working at SSTL in Guildford where, in his friend's words, he is "designing mini-bars for space crafts".

James agrees to pick up car roof bars for Saad's BMW from a seller in Milton Keynes a few weeks later –probably the ones to which Saad strapped the family's bikes when he went to Annecy about 18 months later.

In February 2011 the al-Hillis had a bad fire in the

house. Flames from the wood-burning stove set the chimney ablaze and two fire engines were called to the Claygate property to put it out. Saad tells how he raced back from the SSTL offices in Guildford in record time having got the call from Iqbal. The repair bill and the damage to his home clearly put him under increased strain.

In April of 2011 Saad tells James he is planning to take "the girls" to Europe in the caravan for a week. He says he is "sick of work work work".

When I met James he told me: "Saad was getting fairly stressed. They had a fire caused by a wood-burning stove; the chimney went up. He'd be working in Newhaven, which is quite a long drive, and he would also put the kids to bed. He was trying to rebuild the house as well, while driving five or six hours a day. He was drinking a lot of coffee.

"He had a bad back from lifting an awning on to the back of the house which he'd acquired from a pub, I think! He hadn't got anyone to help him, so I think that was how he did his back in. He was burning out a bit and needed to take some time off, which is why they went off."

Back online a few weeks later he tells how they went to France. He describes it as a "good" break. As well as wanting to recharge his batteries, he makes it clear he went away to be out of the country for the Royal Wedding of Kate Middleton and Prince William.

James told me Saad vehemently opposed some aspects of the British establishment, while appreciating many other facets of the country he always regarded as his own. The last election result, and the austerity cuts that followed David Cameron's arrival at 10 Downing Street, angered him greatly. "He didn't like the ConDems as he called them. He called it an anti-socialist government. It made him talk about going to a different part of Europe because England was going too mercenary. He very much believed in the welfare state and paying your taxes; everybody helping everybody else. He didn't really much like bankers, or people who were very right-wing. He certainly didn't like the Conservatives."

Saad's preoccupation returns to family issues in the next Skype chat. He explains how he has returned from Spain where he was trying to sort out his widowed father Kadhim's problems with a housekeeper who, he claims, has stolen money.

As we have already seen, money was a perennial concern for Saad. He complains that he has spent a lot because of travelling but has failed to earn anything because he had to take unpaid leave. As a freelance contractor he was always watching his bills. In June his worries are assuaged for a while when, he says, his contract at Surrey Satellites Technology Limited (SSTL) is renewed for four months and he is given a better hourly rate.

Hired around 2010 as a freelance sub-contractor for SSTL near Guildford, Saad seemingly enjoyed his professional life there. He was sometimes based at home and tried his hardest to maintain a healthy work-life balance. SSTL designs and launches satellites for private clients, for commercial and security projects. SSTL's corporate work was undoubtedly important, but Saad's role was a modest one. At one point he had been contracted to design the galley area for passenger jets. Saad was a designer who might have done the drawings for a door handle in a defence satellite; he was not someone who designed missile systems.

Later in May Saad tells James he is at home with Zainab because Iqbal has gone to Sweden following the death of her father. "I just have to do the school runs, keep the house, do the shopping, wash Zainab, feed Zainab, do the homework with Zainab.... oh and come to work," he grumbles. The Icelandic volcanic ash cloud threatens to delay his wife's return.

Poignantly, he tells his mate when his father Kadhim passes away on August 11 in a conversation that takes place on September 5, 2011 – precisely one year before his own death. The following day he explains how he has been going back and forth to Spain to make arrangements including bringing his father's body back. He complains about the aggravation of trying to get a death certificate issued in August, which led to the burial at Brookwood Cemetery being delayed for much longer than would normally be the case in keeping with Islamic tradition.

In 2012 the conversations between Saad and James are less frequent, but the banter between the two pals remains the same. They continually switch from sarcastic jokes to serious exchanges about their respective families. In May Saad relates how he was taken to hospital with heart problems and spent five days under observation. Saad says stress is probably the cause of a suspected blockage. He says he is going to take the family away again, for what would turn out to be their last journey together. He offers condolences to James on the death of his mother, and then the Skype log ends with the two words: "good night".

"The last time I heard from him was on

August 28, exactly seven days before he was killed," James recalled. "I had an interview in the industrial estate where SSTL is based, which is where he had been working. I phoned him and he phoned me back and left a voicemail saying he had a bad back and was going to bugger off for a bit. I can still remember the message. My wife didn't like camping; otherwise I might be dead as well. I would happily have gone on holiday with them."

Asked if the holiday had been planned, James replied, "No, I don't think so. He'd booked the first night for the campsite online. I think he intended to use that as a base and then go and find somewhere better."

James claimed Saad told him he also had some business to take care of in Switzerland during the holiday. This was an apparent reference to a Geneva bank account in father Kadhim's name. Annecy was a perfect place to combine relaxation with some personal finance management. As we shall see from further extracts from their conversations, Saad had opened up angrily about the problems this inheritance was causing between him and his brother Zaid.

The day before Saad hooked up the caravan to the tow-bar on his BMW, next-door neighbour

Brian Howells received a call from him to say the family would be going away. Brian himself was in Wales at the time. "He asked me to put the bins out while they were away," he said. "That was the sort of relationship we had."

Asked if he ever noticed anything strange in his neighbours' behaviour, Brian replied: "No, not at all. He got stressed at times, as we all do. We never suspected anything."

He was one of several people Saad spoke to before departure. For a one-week holiday in France, his preparations were fastidious. Saad also called Dr Zaid Alabdi and the pair talked in passing of the feud between Saad and his brother Zaid over "documents" relating to their inheritance.

"I was in the south of France myself that summer," Dr Alabdi told me. "When we came back Saad called me. He told me he was driving to France the following day. He said we should make arrangements to meet up when he got back. I said, 'How is Zaid?' He said, 'Don't go there'. He said he would take all documents because he was worried his brother might get to them. He said not to worry because he had hid them, and then he laughed and said, 'Not even the devil can find them. I hid them really well.' It wouldn't surprise me if he had knocked in a wall and built another one to hide these documents! And then he was gone. That's what happened. Iqbal called to speak to my wife as well. He sent me an email so my wife, who is an accountant, could apply for a job at his firm. He was happy that day, if anything happier than normal."

The night before the family drove down to Dover to take the ferry to France, Jack Saltman was sent an intriguing email from Saad. In the email, which Mr Saltman has not disclosed on the advice of Surrey Police, Saad made allegations about his brother. Mr Saltman said he also expressed direct fears about what might happen to the house in his absence, not explaining whether these fears were to do with his brother or not. Earlier he had asked the neighbour to keep a close eye on the property while the family were away. This was a very normal conversation, just like many people have with neighbours before setting out on a holiday. But when Saad started to make accusations relating to the family feud, Mr Saltman said he wanted something in writing in case there were repercussions.

Mr Saltman explained: "Many months before he had asked for my advice about some family problems. I told him simply to get the best lawyer he could afford. When I spoke to him a few weeks later he said he had hired a family friend. I said I thought that was a mistake. Are you getting totally objective, dispassionate advice? He then told me various things which I found quite disturbing really. Much of it was about his father. About a month later he came with some more problems and again my advice was to go to the lawyer.

"The night before he went to France I was standing out the front and Saad came around the corner. He was certainly very agitated. He said, 'I'm going off to France to give the girls a few more days' holiday before they go back to school'. I asked if they were going to the same place they went to earlier in the year. He said yes. Then he asked me to do certain things. I said I would find it a lot easier if he sent me an email to that effect, which he did ten minutes later. He asked me to keep an eye on his house because from the back of my garden I can the whole of his house. His concern was for the security of his house. That was the last time I saw him. The Thursday afterwards I got a text from my daughter saying, 'Don't the al-Hillis live at the bottom of your garden? They've been murdered'. Shortly after the murders, I gave a hard copy of that email to the police. I no longer have a copy of it."

Julian Steadman had a face-to-face chat with him in the evening, probably a matter of minutes before the BMW rolled off the Oaken Lane driveway for the last time.

"He phoned me in the morning and realised he'd be away at the time the VAT return needed to be sorted," accountant Mr Steadman said. "He rushed around with the books and said, 'Can I leave them with you? I have to go and pick up my mother-in-law from Reading. We are going to France tonight.' They were getting the ferry about ten, I think. I phoned up later and he was rushing around trying to get everything ready to leave at about eight. I nipped round to his house on my bike, and I gave him back the file. That was the last time I saw him. They were literally about to set off for the ferry. I was probably the last person to see him in Claygate."

Chapter 11

First theory: the al-Hilli brothers' bitter feud

From the moment the identities of the Chevaline massacre victims were revealed, one man's name was immediately made public by French police in relation to their enquiries. That man was Saad's older brother Zaid al-Hilli. Suddenly Zaid found himself at the centre of a storm of speculation.

Shy, quiet and mild-mannered, Zaid remains at the time of writing the only person known to have been questioned under caution by police in Britain over the case – one of only a handful anywhere.

Furthermore, Zaid is the only person with whom the assumed principle target of the murderous attack, Saad, was known to have had an acrimonious dispute.

To this day he remains an official suspect in France, a man prosecutor Eric Maillaud would like to be interviewed in Chambery. Zaid, however, steadfastly refuses to cede to the prosecutor's requests.

When I met Monsieur Maillaud in Annecy for this

book, he said: "The sub-hypotheses in this case all concern the al-Hilli family. If we are looking at someone wishing to kill all the family, we are concentrating on the theory centred on the brother Zaid, because we imagine he wanted to be the sole heir of the father."

The prosecutor went on to say the police, despite accumulating boxes of material about the dispute between the two brothers, do not have any actual firm evidence linking Zaid to the murders.

Zaid has seen his life changed for ever since the events of September 5, 2012. Even though it has been proven he cannot be the man who pulled the Luger pistol trigger – the "one bad man" referred to in Zainab's testimony to police – a lingering cloud of suspicion hangs over him. Could he have ordered the executions?

I met Zaid in April 2015 at his flat in Chessington, Surrey, close to the al-Hilli family's home in Claygate. After months of protracted negotiations, he agreed to answer the many questions I had relating to the allegations that have been made against him, particularly those made public by Monsieur Maillaud. It was an interview I never thought would take place.

When he buzzed me into the compact first-floor apartment opposite a Sainsbury's supermarket and a fish restaurant, Zaid was extremely welcoming. He made me a cup of tea and came in from the small kitchen bearing a plate of biscuits. He sat down on the sofa next to me and asked why I was writing a book.

It was little surprise to him when I explained that people continue to be fascinated by the murders of his brother and family in France. As I placed my mug of tea on a small table beside me, I noticed a framed photograph of Saad and Zainab on a shelf. Behind this poignant picture were small black-and-white framed shots of the brothers' parents. On a larger table at the back of the room, in front of a pile of paperback books, were newspaper cuttings about the Chevaline killings which Zaid had kept for reference.

Today Zaid is himself a grandfather-of-three. His only son, Sean, 30, has had three children of his own. There were pictures of the grandchildren and children's DVDs on top of the TV set. He continues to work as a payroll manager for Burhill Group, based at Burhill Golf Club in Walton-on-Thames. The company manages three golf courses across Britain. At work and at home Zaid uses the surname Hilli, rather than al-Hilli.

I thought Zaid might avoid questions and skirt around the incontrovertible evidence that has been put at the heart of the case. But he was happy to answer most of my queries, albeit in a roundabout way on some occasions. His pervading emotion throughout our chat was one of deep anger: anger with the French investigators and Monsieur Maillaud in particular. His disdain for the Annecy prosecutor is impassioned. To Zaid, he and his family are the victims of a cover-up, subject to baseless slurs put out to distract from a shambolic police investigation in France. Yet when pressed about exactly who the authorities are trying to cover for, and why, he struggled to provide me with a definitive response.

Our interview started with some questions about his movements on the day of the killings and in the following days.

Zaid was in Worthing, West Sussex. For most of that Wednesday he was enjoying a day out with a friend in the the south coast resort town. They went for lunch and a stroll along the front, according to Zaid. He has also told how he bought a set of tables in a charity shop that day. The alibi has been checked out by Surrey Police. This confirms Zaid cannot have been the actual gunman.

I asked Zaid where he was when he heard of his brother's death, on September 6. He saw reports of the killings on the breakfast news that morning but claims he made no connection with Saad because the pair were not on speaking terms at the time and, he says, he had no idea his brother's family were in France.

"I was at work," Zaid said. "At 1.15 I usually take a walk at lunchtime. My friend phoned and said I think I have bad news. He said, 'Is Saad's mother-in-law here?' I said, 'I don't know. How should I know?' He said you know what happened in France – I think it's Saad. I said, 'It can't be because his daughter should have started back at school.' I knew because all my grandchildren were going back to school. He said, 'Let me check again.' Then he said, 'It seems like it.' He said he'd been phoning his numbers. I went to the Walton police station which was closed and then went to Esher police station. They put me in touch with Woking police station. They said, 'All we know is what we're hearing.' They asked where I would be and I said I would be going to work to get my stuff. When I got to work they said just go home. I spoke to the police and said I would be waiting at home. Two officers came to see me about 3 o'clock."

It is one of many curious aspects of the case that Zaid – his brother's closest relative and, by his own account, a kindly uncle to Zainab and Zeena - did not immediately fly out to be with the girls at the hospital in Grenoble. He would also probably have been the first person police would have wanted to identify his brother's body.

Most people would surely undertake such a sad journey as an instinctive reaction. Even more so if two little nieces with whom you shared a tight bond desperately needed the comfort of a familiar face. As I was writing this book, following the French Alps aircraft crash, hundreds of relatives of the victims flew out to visit the village nearest the mountain into which the Germanwings jet smashed. They could not even see the place of impact, but they just wanted to be there.

Did you not feel an urge to go, I asked him.

"Yes, because my brother's sister-in-law went," Zaid answered. "I said to the police, 'Am I going as well?' My situation was that I had the press at the front and the back of the building. I couldn't get out. On the Friday they said they would take me out of the flat. They put me somewhere for a couple of days and then they moved me somewhere else in Sussex until things calmed down."

I asked Zaid to explain this in more detail. Did he ask police officers if he could travel to France. I tried to put myself in his situation and decided that if I would definitely have flown, unless I were grounded by the police.

"No, it never occurred to me at that stage," he insisted. "Later on, on the Friday, I said I wanted to go to France and they wouldn't give me an answer. The whole thing was unbelievable."

So who is Zaid al-Hilli, and why were he and his brother, with whom he once shared an exceptionally close bond, so at odds?

As we already know, Zaid and Saad arrived in England in 1971 with their parents. Zaid was 13, three years older than Saad. The two brothers were extremely close. He attended the same central London comprehensive as his younger sibling and the pair moved together with their parents to Claygate.

Friends from the time remember Zaid and Saad as contrasting characters. Zaid was the more serious, while Saad was more of a laugh, practical rather than intellectual. They lived together harmoniously. They went on holidays together, including on trips to the French Alps. Later, the brothers would sometimes collaborate on property investment schemes, buying up houses to renovate and sell on.

"I've met Zaid quite frequently, and I always thought he was a lovely lad," Gary Aked told me. "He was not quite as jovial as Saad, who always wanted to play pranks and lighten the situation. I think Zaid was quite straight-faced. As the older brother he believed the responsibility lay on his shoulders."

In 1985 Zaid had a son with a nurse, Geraldine O'Reilly, 27, a year younger than he was at the time. They later went on to live together in Walton-on-Thames, not far from Claygate. The boy, named Sean, was given the surname O'Reilly-Hilli. Zaid married Geraldine in October 1992 at Fulham register office. The following year Sean's birth was registered in Hammersmith, West London. On the birth certificate Geraldine gave her maiden name, O'Reilly, and gave an address in Ealing, West London as her home. Zaid provided an address in Whitley Bay, Northumberland, as his normal abode. He gave his occupation as a supplies manager.

Tragically, Geraldine died of ovarian cancer in 2007 aged only 49. Zaid had been caring for her throughout her illness and afterwards Saad invited him to stay with his family in Claygate. It must have seemed foolish for Zaid to be grieving alone when he could be in the company of those who cared for him most.

Zaid has spoken happily of that period. In a 2013 interview he told how he would read stories to Zainab and Zeena. Sometimes Saad would visit their father in Spain, leaving his brother to take responsibility for his wife and children, Zaid recalled. Zaid must have been as familiar to the girls as any member of their family when they were both orphaned in France.

During this period, Zaid formed a close bond with Zainab and Zeena.

"I lived there more than a year," he explained to me. "We were very close," he continued. "I would read to them, do paper planes, that sort of thing. The little one would try to get sweets from me! We had a close relationship, and we've kept that."

Relations between the brothers became strained – seemingly irreconcilably – after their dad Kadhim died at his flat in Malaga in August 2011. He had moved to the Costa del Sol to spend his dotage in warmer weather, like many British pensioners, following his separation from the boys' mum.

Saad travelled to Spain to bring back their father's body to be buried alongside their mother in Brookwood Cemetery.

The brothers, sole heirs to Kadhim's estate, also jointly incurred the £15,000 cost of repatriating the body, but Saad told friends he paid the whole bill himself. They have since said this and the fee for the parents' gravestones were trigger points for what became a year of almost continual disagreement. Zaid disagrees.

The argument escalated over the Claygate property, something Zaid willingly accepts. When the boys' mother Fasiha died in 2003, half of the Claygate house was signed over to Zaid – with Saad owning the other half. This was done without there being any disagreement, according to Zaid. A sale would have benefited both brothers but Saad was already living there so they held on to the house, with Zaid half-owning the property his brother was living in.

At one point the stress of the incessant feuding was so bad that Saad ended up in hospital a second time with suspected heart attack symptoms in the months before his death.

Dr Zaid Alabdi remembers Saad being extremely vexed by the strain of continual feuding with his brother and even claims Saad suffered a breakdown in the period.

"Saad took things very seriously," Dr Alabdi said. "At some point before that final holiday he had a nervous breakdown from the trouble and the unfairness he was feeling. I remember once speaking to him on the phone about the problems with his brother and then he started losing his breath and saying, 'I can't talk any more.' His wife told me she had to call an ambulance because he couldn't breathe. I think it had a very big effect on him. He was a pure family man. I couldn't think of anything else that would cause stress."

The first indication of frostiness between the two brothers in the Skype Messenger conversations between Saad and his close friend James Mathews occurred on June 30, 2011. After making reference to a separate person both claim is always after money, Saad commented that this individual "sounds like my brother".

The next remark on the issue comes some three months later. Saad told James he was going to a party at his next-door neighbour's to mark the completion of their extension. In a flippant, off-the-cuff question, Saad's friend asked him if he would be "killing a goat" as well as drinking champagne. Saad quipped that he might "mistake my brother for a goat if I do".

The thorny relationship between the brothers resurfaced in a conversation on Christmas Day evening. This time Saad was much more blatant. Having explained how he had just come back from Malaga with his wife and children where he had been sorting out his father's affairs, he said Zaid is "being an absolute ass hole". The friction in this instance is centred on their father's flat. Saad claimed Zaid already had a 50 per cent stake in the apartment, and now also wanted half of the remainder, giving him a total of 75 per cent. Saad said he had been to see a solicitor and will "no way accept this". Asked more about the dispute, he admitted "we are not talking at all".

In the rest of this Christmas Day Skype chat, seen here in full for the first time, Saad makes a shocking series of allegations about Zaid:

i) Saad claims Zaid made their father sign

a blank Will that was later written so that it disinherited Saad, using false witnesses.

ii) He claims he discovered evidence of alleged fraud and tax evasion by Zaid and threatened to use the information against Zaid if his brother was not "careful".

iii) He claims a family flat in Chessington was bought while Saad was on holiday so that Saad was not on the deeds, and he reveals his fury at Zaid's claim on half the Claygate house that Saad had spent so much time, effort and money doing up.

iv) Saad says he fears that the dispute will end up in court and asks James to act as his witness.

v) He claims antiques and silver went missing from Claygate when Zaid lived there and reveals he had the locks changed to prevent Zaid returning.

vi) He says his brother is not motivated by debts, "just greed".

vi) Finally he claims Zaid is "growing impatient" with the situation and is "doing erratic things".

Here is the full transcript. Sometimes the two talk across each other on the messenger service but the meaning – and the anger – remain clear…

The excerpt starts with another complaint that Zaid went into the family home in Claygate when Saad was not around. Saad, growing increasingly emotional as he strained to get things off his chest, typed that Zaid "just walks in on Iqbal and the kids".

Saad al-Hilli (S a-H): Long story.

James Mathews (JM): Hmmm.

S a-H: But he made a Will for my father that he did not tell me about. All fraud. When my father came last year he asked me where is that paper I signed? I did not know what he was talking about. He made him sign a blank paper.

I found it in the end and there were false witnesses. And I was nowhere mentioned So then I knew what I was in for.

Since then I have been gathering information on brother. A lot of fraud … tax evasion and so on. I am shocked at the information I have gathered. Can he really be my brother!!!

JM: But you don't need to use the info...

S a-H: I will if he does not be careful. I put half this house in his name when my mother died. And now he wants me to buy it from him. 400K. When he has put zero £ in it.

JM: You have done a lot of work.

S a-H: And all my work and earning have gone in this house... U know how hard I have worked in it. Yes and he says I will pay for none of it.

Please be there in court to tell them when I need you. Because I think this is where it will end up.

JM: If you need me there I will tell what I have seen.

S a-H: Thanks. He has turned out to be a right shit... what can I say.

JM: It is a shame when money causes family fights!

S a-H: My offer was to take the Spanish flat of my father's... take my half of the Chessington flat... and with the 200K my father has given u [Zaid] in the past that should settle it... just put back the house in my name.

JM: Sounds fair.

S a-H: Nope. He has taken all the flat in Chessington as he bought it when I was away on holiday and I found out I was not even on the deeds. He is willing to take 3/4 of the flat in Spain. And he says father has given me nothing.

JM: Which implies that Father thought you had all the big house?

S a-H: But I have proved he has as I have found all the back statements of my father... it has been hard looking for the last 7 months.

JM: Or it would to a lawyer

S a-H: Anyway he is getting impatient and is doing erratic things now.

JM: Has he got debts then?

S a-H: A lot of evidence... I had to [think] he has thought this out for years... since 1998 and has the law with him on documents. No, renting a place apparently in Walton. He even forged my signature on a trusted deed I found in his boxes.

JM: That is not good.

S a-H: That apparently my mother made. But I went to see the witness and asked was I there when she signed... no, your brother just brought the paper round, she said. That was made in 1998.

JM: It seems crazy to try to hurt his brother.

S a-h: Hmmm yes I am still shocked really. And feel used. Very. Especially with what I have done for him. When he left I changed the locks to the house as antiques and silver has now disappeared. No debts... just greed.

JM: So sad.

S a-H: And now he want to take action regarding the locks.

Excerpt from transcript of Skype conversation between Saad al-Hilli and James Mathews, Christmas Day 2011.

Zaid's version of events, as one would expect, is contrasting. Sat on the sofa in his flat, wearing his office clothes but with his shoes taken off, he addressed his brother's accusations. He freely admits there was a feud which meant he and Saad were only communicating through lawyers in the 11 months leading up to the murders. He contends the argument was just about Claygate, worth a lot of money, upwards of £800,000. But it also has also been alleged that it extended to the rest of Kadhim's estate – a bank account in Geneva containing an estimated €1million (£720,000) and his flat in Spain, said to be worth about £80,000? .

I asked him to explain why he and Saad were not speaking to each other.

"We were doing it through a lawyer," Zaid confirmed. "Unfortunately that didn't work out. I changed lawyers at the end. We left it at that. I'm still a person who, if I don't want to communicate with someone, I just don't want to know. I'll do it through the proper legal process. That's all it was. Disagreement is merely about one thing: Saad wanted the house that he was living in, my share, to give it him. I've left it to him in a will, but I wasn't prepared to give it to him there and then."

The dispute rumbled on without resolution, Zaid explained. Both brothers had the same lawyer, a friend of the family, who he wanted to act as a mediator. But Zaid felt she took his brother's side, so he had to seek another solicitor to advise him.

"I had no problem with it," he insisted, referring again to the house situation. "I never asked them for rent or anything like that because I know he liked to live there and I was happy with that. He was happy; I was happy. I was not going to ask him to get a mortgage just to pay me. I wouldn't do it. I said, 'I'm not giving it to you now. It's in my will. If I'm gone, you'll have it'."

He wanted it at that very moment?

"Yes, which I wasn't prepared to do at the time," Zaid replied to me. "That is the main disagreement. I could have taken him to court and I would have forced a sale and that sort of thing, but I didn't. I gave him a proposal, a very, very fair price for my share. I was willing to keep him happy but unfortunately he didn't accept it. I think I did my best."

Zaid then said "unfortunately this happened", meaning the murders, adding "and at the wrong time as well, for everybody".

Saad and Zaid had not spoken since a violent confrontation while Zaid was still living at Claygate, on the evening of October 2, 2011. Police were called to the house, Zaid told me. It is the first time he has spoken in such graphic detail of this particular episode that brought the simmering tensions to the surface.

"All I asked him is for something and he reacted," he claimed. "I went up to my bedroom and he came back, charging – he's a much bigger guy than I am – and he

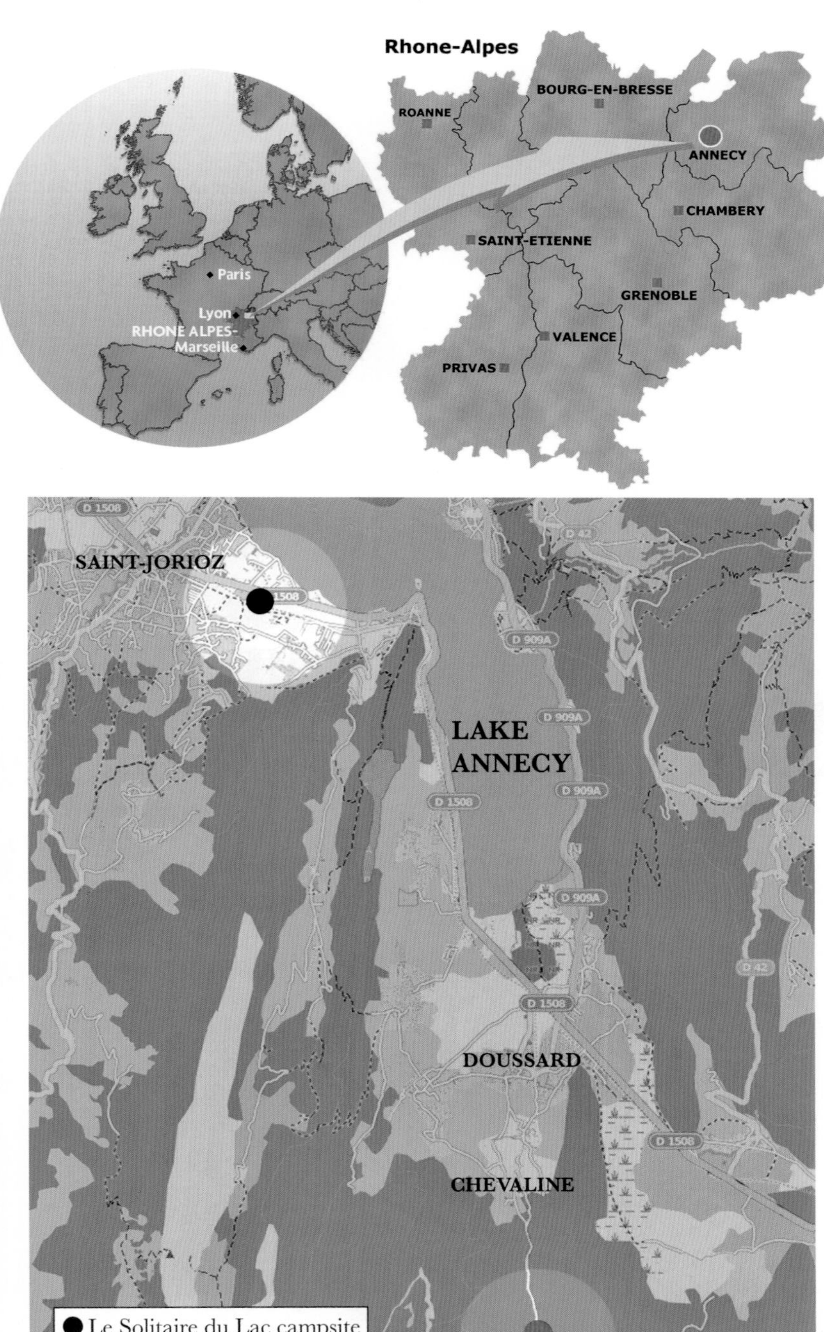

The maps above show the location of the campsite on the shores of Lake Annecy, as well as the remote location of the killings.

BRIT FAMILY GUNNED DOWN IN FRANCE

Carjackers kill 4 and leave girl of 8 fighting for life

Above and below: The al-Hilli's bullet-riddled BMW pictured at the crime scene, the Le Martinet lay by.

BRIT GROUP DIE IN FRENCH MASSACRE

HOLS VICTIMS WERE RIDDLED WITH BULLETS

Family blasted at remote Alps beauty spot

THE 'VENICE OF ALP

Above: and right: The Daily Mirror reports on the brutal murders.

Above and below left and right: The al-Hilli family were staying at the Solitaire du Lac campsite on the shores of Lake Annecy in France.

Above: Saad al-Hilli

ALPS MASSACRE: AGONY OF GIRL, 4, AS KILLERS HUNTED

THE HOUSE

THE CAMPSITE

THE CAR

WHERE IS MUMMY? ..I WANT MUMMY

– FOUR-YEAR-OLD ZEENA

THE MURDER SCENE

VICTIMS

Police facing an extremely difficult task

ANALYSIS

Above: Daily Mirror. September 7, 2012.

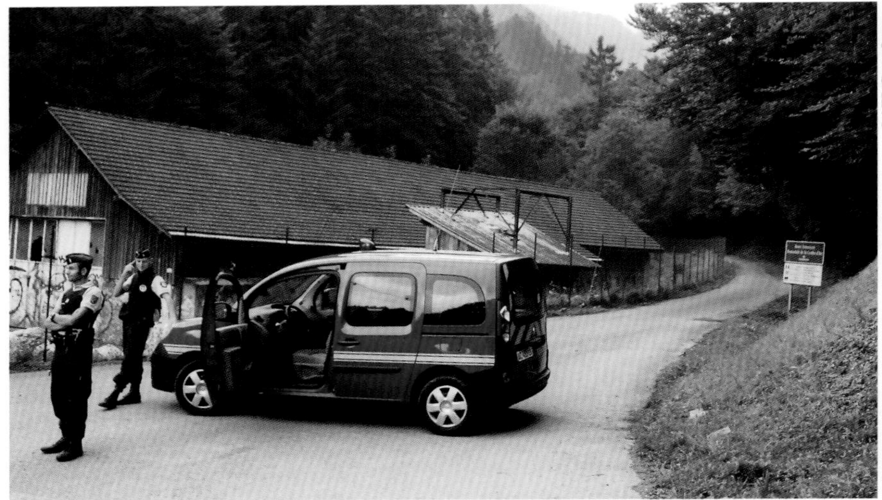

Above: Gendarmes guard the entrance to the Route Forestière Domaniale de la Combe d'Ire - the remote road leading up to the Le Martinet lay-by.

Above: The road into the tranquil village of Chevaline.

Above: TV crews set up in the remote surroundings.

Above: The world's press visit Le Martinet lay-by, where the shootings took place.
Inset: Author, and Daily Mirror reporter, Tom Parry visits the scene.

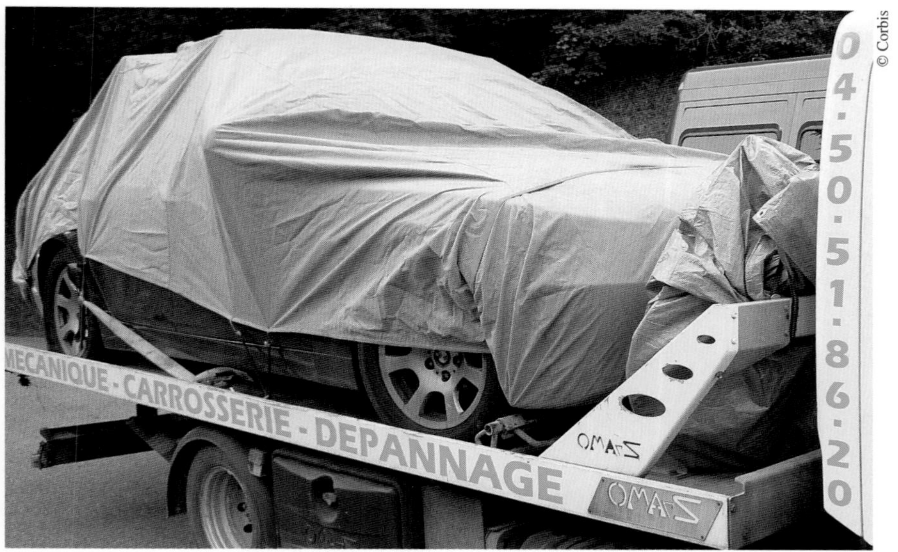

Above: The al-Hillis' BMW is taken away from the crime scene.

Above: French cyclist Sylvain Mollier was also killed.

Above: Sylvain was a production worker at the nuclear metal factory, Cezus, at the far edge of Ugine.

Above: Police released an e-fit of a motorcyclist. He was later cleared.

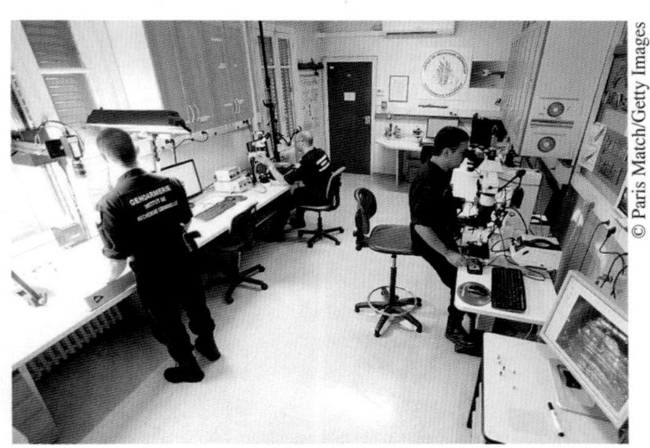

Above: Forensic teams worked around the clock to find evidence.

Above: Iqbal (back row, centre) studied dentistry at the University of Baghdad, Iraq.

Above: Iqbal was previously married to James 'Jimmy' Thompson in the USA.

Above: Iqbal with Jimmy's sister, Judy Weatherly in New Orleans.

Above: When Iqbal lived in the USA, she was known as Kelly.

© Tom Parry

Above: The al-Hilli home in Claygate, Surrey.
Below right: One of Saad's self-built sheds and garden-storage areas.

© Tom Parry

Left: Saad's brother, Zaid al-Hilli speaks exclusively to Tom.

Above: Tom Parry interviews French Prosecutor Eric Maillaud.

Right: Eric Maillaud.

Below: Didier Berthollet, Chevaline's mayor at the time.

pinned me down on the bed and he calls his wife and says, 'He's hitting me, he's hitting me.'" Zaid laughs at this memory. "I was underneath. He told her to phone the police. She said, 'No, what are you talking about', but he went and phoned the police. The policewoman said, 'Look, I'm not interested in any of this, it's only because of the children here.' I was planning to go out for the day and that's it. I was looking for a property, a flat to move into, as well, so I was getting myself ready to move out, and I think that was an impetus to move out. It's very unfortunate because we were very close. We went on holiday together and all sorts of things, lots of trips to Brighton so many times, you know. It's just a shame."

Zaid claims that when he returned some time later to collect some belongings his brother had changed the locks.

This has been previously confirmed by a relative of the brothers who made public a letter from Saad dated September 16, 2011 – almost a year to the day before the murders. Mae Faisal El-Wailly, a childhood friend of Saad and Zaid, revealed that the younger brother had written to her a month after their father died.

"Zaid and I do not communicate any more as he is another control freak and tried a lot of underhanded things even when my father was alive," Saad wrote. "He tried to take control of father's assets and demanded control. It's a long story and now I have just had to wipe him out of my life. Sad but I need to concentrate now on my wife and two lovely girls."

Despite the letter, Mrs El-Wailly, who had moved to Arizona in the US from Iraq, did not believe the row could have escalated into a planned murder.

As Saad's message log shows, there were also other causes of friction as far as the younger brother was concerned. I asked Zaid about all of them.

As regards the cost of repatriating their father's remains, he said: "No. We paid the money. I paid some of it on my card but couldn't do all of it so he paid the rest and sorted things out. I asked him, 'Please can we settle this bill?' because I know I owed him money. He wouldn't talk to me then. I said, 'Look this can be done tonight, let's sort it out.' It was £1,200 I owed him. I gave him that money. I don't see why there was any disagreement."

I also asked Zaid about Saad's inference he had stolen antiques before he was able to change the locks. What do you say about that, I asked?

"Lies," he replied, laughing bitterly as he said it. "We are trying to find them now. I've never had them. They were in the house. I don't know where they are; that's the problem. You can ask the police!"

In relation to the Chessington flat, he told me there was no disagreement. There is also no evidence whatsoever that Zaid has committed fraud or tax evasion, or that Saad threatened that he would make his claims about this public.

I also asked him to respond to Saad's

comment to James Mathews that "he made a will for my father which he didn't tell me about".

Zaid's reply was in the present tense. "Well, look, Saad knows the truth and his allegations have proved to be all nonsense. As I say, unfortunately, because I did not hand the keys of the house to him he started coming up with all this. Erm, it is very unfortunate that he went down that route and he shouldn't have because, you know, it's not right. He knew about everything; Saad was aware of everything."

Asked about the claim from Saad that he allegedly made their father sign a blank paper with false witnesses, he said: "Well, one minute he's saying my father signed it, because he knew about it and Saad knew about it as well," he answered. "No, unfortunately, no false witnesses. Nothing like that. To wrap it up, er, my signatures were taken and everything came back in my favour so, all these allegations are nonsense basically."

Probate papers have shown that on August 8, 2011 Saad had taken the step of putting a block on his father's Will. The block, known as a caveat, meant that the terms of the Will could not go ahead by February 2013 at the earliest. It essentially paused any claim Zaid might have over the fortune.

I asked Zaid to confirm whether their father had left a Will or not.

"The only Will was that what he had signed," Zaid replied. "But Saad didn't want to use it. Fine, he didn't want to use it."

Zaid's suggestion contradicts the notion that this was Saad trying to block him getting at the money in Geneva. He instead says they both agreed to freeze the account. The money, Zaid says, was savings their father brought with him from his business in Iraq. The account was opened in 1988, some years after they left the country. He says he is unable to access the money in the account to this day because it is going "through the legal process". Zaid also claims to not know how much is in the account.

"That account was frozen from the day my father went to hospital because he isn't capable to deal with it," he said. " So for anyone to say he's going to access it – well, how do you access anything like that?"

Asked who froze the account, he added: "The bank itself. We informed them that my father was ill, he's had a stroke. They said, 'We'll freeze it'. We didn't want anybody to access it. He had a carer and all that. What they [carers] know, we don't know."

The Swiss prosecutor, Dario Zanni, alleged Zaid had tried to use a credit card, I reminded him. Mr Zanni told a Swiss newspaper he fraudulently attempted to acquire two credit cards which would have given him access to the money in the account.

"No, my father did apply for these," Zaid replied. "He was here when he applied. That was the only matter."

In the same article, published a year after the murders,

Mr Zanni said: "Heritage is probably the knot of the problem. We are certain that the two brothers were trying to neutralise each other to be certain that neither one of them could get their hands on the money."

Mr Zanni alleged Zaid contacted the bank in July 2012 asking for assurance that Saad had not obtained any of the cash. When I spoke to Zaid he dismissed all of these suggestions as "nonsense".

"He's talking rubbish," he continued. "These people, I don't know why they make it up. Do they just want to be in the news these people? My French lawyer said these people want these 15 minutes of fame."

Zaid also rejected the claim that on September 3, 2012 – just two days before he died – Saad called the bank to forewarn them of his next visit. He was said to be extremely disturbed when he made the call. According to Zaid, Saad would never have made such a call because he knew the account was frozen.

Saad's accountant Julian Steadman, however, remembers his client telling him about what was going on "in the family" during one of their regular meetings to go through VAT returns and that Saad had kept a record of their conversations. "He told me about the problems with his brother," Mr Steadman said. "Saad recorded what had been going on and I think police have been able to get it off the hard drive."

The simmering and intractable dispute was brought to an abrupt closure by the murders of September 5

2012. As far as Zaid is concerned though, any discussion of what he hoped would always remain private, between members of his own family, is "all nonsense", a distraction from the real police investigation.

Chapter 12

The stand-off: Zaid al-Hilli and the French police

Zaid was arrested on June 24, 2013, on suspicion of ordering the Alps killings. The actual charge was conspiracy to commit murder. Nine plain clothes officers spent a day searching his Chessington flat. They took away bags of evidence. Zaid was interviewed for the whole day and held overnight in police cells in nearby Guildford. He was released on police bail while further enquiries were conducted.

It seemed the French investigators must have told the British officers they had at last obtained evidence that would enable them to charge their number one suspect. Prosecutor Eric Maillaud had never made any secret of his view that the explanation for the Chevaline mystery lies in Britain, not in France.

On the day of Zaid's arrest, Monsieur Maillaud said: "The arrest confirms that the family is the most interesting line of enquiry. Formal and written evidence leaves no doubt about the very violent family dispute that pitted the two brothers on the issue of the inheritance of their father. There are very specific questions which need to be asked about it. We need to ask him questions about his schedule at the time, his relationship with his brother and the family inheritance."

The background to the out-of-the-blue arrest, it is now clear, was Zaid's refusal to comply with the French investigators' demands. He was ordered in 2013 to travel to France for questioning but refused. He has said that he was afraid to go and that he had already completed 25 hours of witness interviews and felt he had nothing left to say. When I spoke to Zaid in April, he told me it is actually 30 hours of police interview. However, because of his refusal, under his lawyer's direction, to go to France he received a formal summons to be questioned by police in the Alpine city of Chambéry, where the main inquiry team is based. After ignoring this summons he was arrested at home.

"I was offered by the British police the chance to meet Maillaud," Zaid told me. "I didn't take it up. One of them said he would come with me to France as a reassurance. This was a British police superintendent overseeing the whole thing. He was the one who said to me I was a victim myself. But everybody advised me not to. I really didn't feel like going. The French police are here. If they want to interview me, they can come here. Why should I go there?"

Monsieur Maillaud has previously alleged that answers Zaid gave at the beginning of their inquiries were evasive and contradicted what he later said. In particular, he pointed out that Zaid initially told British police assigned to the case that his relationship with his brother was fine. This was a comment allegedly repeated in media interviews too. Only later, some time after the killings, did Zaid confess he and Saad had a long-standing dispute – although not one grave enough for him to have ever contemplated taking his brother's life, he said.

In January 2014, six months after the arrest, Surrey Police announced that Zaid's bail conditions were being lifted. "At this stage there is insufficient evidence to charge him with any criminal offence and no further action is being taken at this time," a spokesman said. There was seemingly no meaningful evidence which enabled prosecutors to press charges.

Since then there has been nothing substantial

enough to transform festering suspicions still held by the French investigators into categorical proof sufficiently strong enough to be put before a judge and jury.

This is something Monsieur Maillaud confirmed to me. "Looked at objectively, we have no firm evidence linking Zaid to the murders," he said. "That's the truth."

The Surrey Police statement was hardly a ringing endorsement, but it at least enabled Zaid to return to some kind of normality. In a highly unusual staged photo-call, Zaid shook hands with a senior Surrey Police detective outside Guildford police station. This was pure PR, a photograph aimed at telling the media Zaid had a clean bill of health.

The French prosecutor, however, was quick to remind Zaid that investigators there were still convinced of his involvement in foul play, saying on the same day: "In France we would probably not have lifted them [the bail conditions]. But procedures are different in other countries. This does not mean that we are finished with Zaid al-Hilli or that he is innocent. His status remains that of a suspect. He could be questioned again if the joint French-British investigation team decides that it is necessary."

In our interview, Monsieur Maillaud made one

particularly stark remark about Zaid. He admitted the elder al-Hilli brother "must look at me as the devil incarnate", but then went on to allege: "There are other members of the family who are convinced it was Zaid who killed his brother and they have even said so to the investigators."

The impasse between Monsieur Maillaud and Zaid is one that cannot be bridged. Neither man has met the other in person, but Zaid in particular is furious at how his reputation has been so consistently tarnished by the prosecutor. I asked him for his honest opinion about the Frenchman, and he didn't hold back in his highly personal assessment of the lawyer.

"Well he's an idiot basically," he stated before adding, bizarrely, "I think in North Korea, he'd do very well there!"

"For a prosecutor to come out so soon and point fingers before an investigation has started; well, he's not a prosecutor, he's a complete fool," he continued. "He probably pretends to be a fool but I think he's more than that. I think he's a scoundrel.

"Some of this material that he has come up with sounds like Eric Cantona," he went on. "I mean you just don't understand what he's talking about!"

Zaid also compared the French investigators

unfavourably to recent high-profile cases like the murder of Anni Dewani in South Africa, in which speculation has not been relied on by the trial judge.

"This man is actually twisting the facts," Zaid concluded, becoming exasperated as he explained his position to me. "He is using all that to justify what they are doing. We knew it wasn't going to go anywhere. Just give it time and it will collapse. It was heading off a cliff. For us what was happening was we were angry and frustrated that the attention has been focused on the UK without a shred of evidence. Just mere speculation from the prosecutor and the police and the judges. That whole thing should have been wrapped up in a month. The UK has got nothing to do with it."

Ask Saad's friends about whether Zaid could have ordered the killings and the response is unanimous. I was unable to get a ringing endorsement from any of them, but none believed he would be capable of hiring a contract killer.

"I'd always thought his mother had bequeathed the whole house to Saad," Gary Aked said. "When I heard that Zaid wanted part of it my reaction was 'greedy bastard'. I mean Zaid has loads of properties, he has millions of pounds; there's nothing he wants.

I think he was just getting a bit greedy. Saad had told me his brother was a bit of a money-grabber, and he hadn't said it with a smile. That was the only thing they disagreed on. Zaid wanted some of the house, or the money from the sale of the house I think, but if it wasn't for Saad it wouldn't have been in one piece. It needed a lot of work doing on it. People I know said to me Zaid sounds dodgy. I agreed he does come across like that, but I still think he's innocent. I do not believe there is any way he would put a hit on his brother. I think it's too far-fetched. Absolutely no way Zaid would have done that. He was money-orientated; it was engrained in him. I think because he was the older brother he thought the money should have gone to him."

Dr Zaid Alabdi used to talk with Saad about his relationship with his brother. Remembering these conversations, he said: "As my name is Zaid like his brother he always used to say to me: 'The two important people in my life both have the same name.' I never met Zaid until Saad's funeral. I heard he is a very complex person. With Saad when his name came up he would always change the subject. According to Saad he was one of those people who are in love with money; he wanted money as much as possible. I was told he was not someone who wanted to spend it on holidays and cars; he always bought flats to buy and sell them. The mother gave the house to Saad, according to him. He told me that he told Zaid that he would like to give half of it to his brother when she died. The problem started with the dad, he said; when he claimed he found out his brother was taking money from the dad. That triggered a big problem. You are dealing with someone who is in love with money. Then the dad died and problems got worse. He left them money in Geneva in a bank account. He left them a few flats. They both had a flat shared between them from when they were at university. Saad said when it came to sharing Zaid took the flat because it was in his name, but also wanted half of the house. You can see there is a lot of unfairness."

Dr Alabdi added: "But there is nothing violent about the brother. I think he is just greedy. For me it sounds very illogical that he has done this."

James Mathews provided a far from glowing tribute of Zaid, but he said: "I genuinely don't think Zaid was capable of organising a murder whatever I think of his character."

Another person I spoke to was Geraldine's brother, Damien O'Reilly, based in Walton-on-Thames. Zaid's former brother-in-law said: "I haven't spoken to Zaid for a long time, but that's just what happens when families drift apart. There is no way that Zaid would have been involved in anything like this. I never thought he could have done anything to harm anyone and it seems to have come to fruition. All the investigations don't seem to have led anywhere and I'm not surprised by that."

Zaid, meanwhile, remains absolutely convinced that his relatives were not the real targets. He is firmly of the view that the cyclist, Sylvain Mollier, was the intended victim, and that the British-Iraqi family were, as a vocal few have claimed all along, normal holidaymakers in the wrong place at the wrong time. He has always maintained that the idea he could arrange a contract killing in the French Alps is absurd.

"I love my brother. I love his family. I love my nieces; I would never harm them," he once insisted.

Speaking of the French investigators, he informed me: "I think they knew exactly who was the target, and it was Sylvain Mollie. I have the feeling that this guy, somebody wanted him out of the way. Whether the French authorities know about it beforehand and the whole thing went wrong and they have to cover it up quite quickly, or they had to cover it up afterwards.

I think there were important people involved in his killing."

I asked him who he meant by that. "Somebody important in the area," he replied. He went on to allege that Monsieur Maillaud must be covering up for someone else, a higher ranking official.

"I think it was politically-motivated, the whole thing," he said later when asked to define his views on the why the culprit might have targeted Mollier. " I mean locally; I think there are people that are involved in it locally."

Zaid has repeatedly accused the French police of incompetence. He said a series of blunders had convinced him they did not know what they were doing. Their failure to secure the crime scene, which was "trashed" by emergency services vehicles, was one alleged failing.

"We didn't have any faith in the investigation," Zaid told me. "We knew it was not going anywhere. They compromised the integrity of this investigation. Once you lose trust in it how are you going to find the truth? I don't think we will ever find out. First of all the crime scene wasn't properly protected from what I understand. It was actually trashed."

"If the gendarmerie are not capable of conducting the investigation, it says it all," Zaid persisted. "If you cannot secure the crime scene, they could have called on any organisation to investigate it properly but they failed. The crime scene was trodden over, ambulances and fire engines were let through, the police were all over it; it was contaminated. Apparently, from what I understand, there are hit after hit after hit of contamination."

Another failing, Zaid has claimed, was the inability to retrieve Saad's passport for a long time.

"We were told that the French police had found a passport and they claim that they found a passport in my brother's jacket," Zaid declared. "It seems that the jacket had been in the lab for a year-and-a-half and no one bothered to search it. So what other evidence have they missed?"

From Zaid's perspective, the whole investigation has been a witch-hunt which resorted to "smears and lies" against the family.

The French police were drip-feeding information to the press to forever stain their good name, he claimed.

"As a family we don't trust them; we have no faith in them," he said. "Once you mishandle something it is very difficult to build that trust again. What they did wasn't right at all. The judges have said mistakes were made but is this just to placate us?

"The French were looking for every little thing," he went on, describing the years of police inquiries. "The French rely on racial profiling to perpetuate their lie. Unfortunately that didn't get them anywhere and they knew that was not going to get them anywhere, from the beginning. So, that's why we are, at this point, this investigation is being handled incompetently and by people who are not serious about looking for the culprits, although I think they know who did it, who the culprits are."

It is Zaid's contention that the French police decided from day one that Sylvain Mollier could not be the target. From my investigations, however, I can say that Zaid is incorrect in this assertion. The French police have never dismissed the theory that the cyclist could have been the target. In fact, they have been able to conduct a far fuller investigation into that line of inquiry than any other because they are within an hour's drive of most relevant associates of Sylvain Mollier.

Zaid remains a man on a mission, a mission to establish his version of the truth. He is more determined than ever. As well as being arrested and kept on bail, he also endured an interrogation he believes is linked to his suspect status while on holiday in Hong Kong. He told how he was taken to one side and into a side room when he got to border control during a visit to Macau on a trip to the Far East last year. Officers questioned him for seven hours, saying he was a "witness" to a crime. They had a photograph of him, which he believes is confirmation the police sent his details to police forces around the world in case he tried to disappear. He says he was on a "blacklist".

I can reveal he has recently hired a French lawyer to obtain copies of the case files so he can prove his contentions. "I just want to see what he comes up with," he told me. "It's going to take a long time. I don't understand the process. We'll see how it goes."

Zaid is at still firmly at odds with Monsieur Maillaud who says he too is determined to get to the bottom of this most incomprehensible crime. The French prosecutor continues to make it abundantly clear he sincerely believes Zaid knows more than he has told British police. One year on from the crime being committed, the prosecutor said: "It's true that he presents an interesting profile as he is animated by a feeling of hate and vengeance."

When I spoke to Monsieur Maillaud for this book, he remained convinced that there were questions over Zaid, how he initially co-operated, but then refused to comply with the investigators' wishes. But he maintained they were certain of nothing, except that the case was still a mystery.

"We cannot find another member of the al-Hilli family who would have wanted rid of Saad al-Hilli apart from Zaid," he said. "We have not found any suspicious movements in relation to Zaid either. But, in considering Zaid being capable of ordering the murder of his brother and his nieces, there are as many question marks as there about any other motive. If he had paid an assassin to do this, why did the assassin not finish the job? He might have thought he had killed Zainab because she fainted from the blow of being pistol-whipped, but if someone had been paid by Zaid, and followed them from a distance, he would have seen clearly that the other little girl got in the car. Why didn't he kill her? The investigators have wondered whether after a certain point he had just had enough. It's possible he said to himself, 'Enough is enough, I'm not killing children.' And then he left."

At the British inquest into the Annecy deaths in November 2014, Zaid was one of only a handful of people to give evidence. He confirmed details of his brother's life before he was killed. Interestingly, he said that both he and Saad had been to the area with their parents when they were children. The coroner in Woking found that the family members had been unlawfully killed.

This was news to no one. The question everyone wanted an answer to was of course: if they were unlawfully killed, then who killed them?

Chapter 13

Second theory: Iqbal's secret American husband

In a case full of unexpected twists, probably the most bizarre of all emerged in 2014, from the United States. The investigation had already taken in Britain, France, Switzerland, Sweden and Iraq, and many more countries besides. Here was a location that the baffled Annecy murder squad never for a second believed might be relevant to their lengthy enquiries. That was until they began to probe Iqbal's life prior to her coming to Britain in 2003.

Until this point the focus of the investigation, and most news stories, had always been Saad. Then the French authorities revealed to the media for the first time that not only did Iqbal have a secret husband in New Orleans, but also that man, Jimmy Thompson, died the very same day as the al-Hillis –

September 5, 2012.

The 60-year-old's abrupt death from an apparent heart attack happened 5,000 miles away in his home state of Mississippi. He died at the wheel of his red pick-up truck as he drove home from his antiques business in Natchez. Angry motorists sounded their horns while his vehicle sat motionless at traffic lights until someone though to check on the driver.

Dad-of-three Jimmy, who had high blood pressure, had felt ill all day and was looking grey, it was reported at the time. In the antiques shop he complained of pain in his chest and arm.

This was, though, an uncanny coincidence. Only a few hours separated the deaths of the former spouses who seemingly hadn't contacted each other in nearly 12 years.

In Annecy, Lt-Col Vinnemann was not exaggerating when he said: "We have discovered some astonishing things."

Iqbal's time in the US was "shrouded in mystery," he claimed.

As has already been demonstrated through my interviews with those who knew her there, it can be established that Iqbal was for a time happy with Jimmy and was reluctant to leave. In his statement, Lt-Col Vinnemann did, however, state that the short relationship was "never spoken about" at the al-Hilli home in Surrey.

The bombshell announcement was enough to prompt some of Jimmy's relatives to claim he had been killed by a poison dart. They had never believed the official explanation of a heart attack. The suggestion the two deaths might have been co-ordinated hits ordered by a secret enemy corresponded with their view that his demise was due to foul play. His daughter Joy Martinolich voiced her concerns.

Joy, from Rhode Island, on the US Eastern Seaboard, insisted most of the family had questioned the coroner's findings after her father's death. "If you wanted to kill somebody and get away with it you would do something that people would accept, like a heart attack," she said. "They would accept he was a bit overweight, that he had stress issues, he was pushing 60. It's possible. My aunt said, in the middle of her grief, that someone had said something about a dart. She thought a couple of people had said something about poison, that this was not a heart attack."

Others were far less suspicious, however, accepting that the very odd timing of Jimmy and Iqbal's deaths were uncanny, spooky even, but nothing more than that.

Sabah Alshaikhly downplayed the imputation of foul play. There could be no direct relation between the deaths of the former spouses on either side of the Atlantic, he insisted.

"The two deaths are hard to understand; but they are just an unbelievable coincidence," was his explanation when contacted in July 2014. "Coincidences can happen," he went on. "Jim died of natural causes, of a heart attack. He had a very unhealthy diet. He ate fried chicken, hamburgers, fries. I said to him, 'this is going to kill you', and he replied, 'but at least I'll die happy'. Three months later he was dead. If he had been killed by a gun, I would have said, investigate, but he died naturally."

Interviewed earlier about the moment he heard what had happened to Iqbal, he said: "I was very surprised and upset when I heard of her death. I am sure her death had nothing to do with anyone in America. It is very sad, but I know the answer to this mystery is not here. We would have nothing to gain by killing that beautiful lady. We all loved and respected her and we were incredibly upset by the news she passed. She was far too young. We left on good terms and there was no bad blood. Jim loved her."

It had been more than a decade since Iqbal,

AKA Kelly, had left the US. Not that long afterwards, in Abu Dhabi, she met Saad. If she had told him about her ex, he must have accepted it. Regardless, 12 years had passed since she and Jimmy had gone their separate ways and detectives would have struggled to find a substantial connection that might have motivated simultaneous murders by unknown co-ordinated enemies thousands of miles apart.

For a long time it seemed there was no evidence of lingering contact between the separated couple who had lived together in America. Dr Alabdi told me that one reason he ruled this out was that Iqbal made out she was terrified of using the internet.

"Saad used to laugh at Iqbal when she said she didn't want an email address," Dr Alabdi said. "She would say, 'What if people know where I am?' Maybe she wanted not to be known."

But Judy Weatherly has revealed to me for the first time that this was not the case. Iqbal and Jimmy, she claims, were in regular contact via email after Iqbal moved to the UK with Saad.

"I saw emails between him and Kelly at the time he sent them, after she had gone over to England," Judy claimed. "He'd go up to his room and he'd tell me, but then I didn't pay that much attention. I said he should keep it to himself because it could cause her a lot of trouble at her end. He said, 'Yeah, I know', because she had told us that. She told us that before she left. I had said, Can you write us?' She said, 'I'll keep up with everybody through Jim'. He didn't have her as a friend on Facebook but they would email each other. She definitely did keep in touch with my brother.

"Jim didn't even tell his friends that she and him were still talking to each other. He didn't even tell his best friend Nick. He never would talk about Kelly. He didn't want anything to get back to her in any kind of way. Jim was a very paranoid kind of person. He was scared of being overheard. He never talked about her except to me."

One can imagine that Saad might well have been angry if he had discovered these alleged exchanges between Iqbal and her previous husband, whom she might not even have told him about. But for the purposes of the investigation the question remains: why would an individual or organisation bear a grudge against both Jimmy and Iqbal, on opposite sides of the Atlantic, 12 years after they went their separate ways?

Judy also told me that Jimmy made an odd request to a niece about two weeks before his death.

He had warned that if anything happened to him his family should go through his room. "There is something there that will surprise you," Judy claims her brother told her daughter. After he died they honoured the request and found a box in the back of a wardrobe containing photographs of his wedding to Iqbal, as well as their wedding and divorce papers. Did this amount to anything more than souvenirs of a happy time? Was there something more sinister at play?

Jimmy's family only found out about the Alps massacre via the authorities. "There was nothing over here about it," Judy told me. "When I was coming back from New Orleans to Mississippi one time that's when I found out. The FBI contacted me. I was so upset at the time about my brother dying that I wouldn't even talk to them. I had to get James's best friend to call them back because I couldn't talk to them. When I found out that she died, especially so tragically, it just pulled me apart. It had been years since I'd heard from her or talked to her but I knew that she and Jim had still been communicating. He told me the French authorities got in touch with them and he was international FBI. They wanted to know about exhuming him, and we told them no. Then we didn't hear anything, and then it was on the news about a year later when the French police released it to the media. For a long time we had kept it quiet because we didn't want to talk about it."

Judy was too upset to do much in the immediate aftermath of Jimmy's death. She was grief-stricken, not only from losing him but also her other brother. Shortly afterwards her mother died. Only when her grief lessened did she decide to check his emails, and that was when she became suspicious.

"At first I didn't think anything," she continued. "He was slightly overweight, but he wasn't obese or anything like that. We didn't have an autopsy done. He had been feeling great. A few months later when I was trying to get my head straight because I was missing him so much, I tried to check his emails to see who had been contacting him. After the FBI called me I checked again and they were all gone. They were gone from midnight backwards. The password had been changed too. I had set it all up. It really started bothering me all over again. I really thought something funny was going on. Somebody erased all his email. Jim didn't erase anything. He would say, 'You never know when you might want to go back and check something out.' I had set it all up for him, I had set up the password; he didn't even have it. I had set up his Facebook account too. There were things in there that they wanted to see. They wanted to see if him and Iqbal were talking. They wanted to see what they were saying, that kind of thing."

Since being contacted by the FBI, Judy has become increasingly convinced there was "more going on" than first seemed the case on September 5, 2012. She even claims there was an attempt on Jimmy's life a few weeks before he died when a woman jumped in front of him while he was out on his motorcycle.

And now for the first time she has spoken about what she believes is much more than just a sinister coincidence. In the weeks after the news emerged in 2014, Judy tried to hide from the media, although she did do some interviews. She claims she desperately wanted to shield her and Jimmy's elderly father from the speculation. Now Judy wants the full story of what happened to both Jimmy and Iqbal to be properly uncovered. So far, she is not satisfied with the answers.

"I really think that her life here had a lot to do with the murder," Judy told me. Probe a little further, though, and it is difficult to establish precisely why that would be so. There are mutterings of strange happenings, but nothing that could form a prosecution case in a court of law.

It certainly appears that this was another implausible lead: too odd to be ignored, but actually going nowhere. A few days after Lt-Col Vinnemann made his announcement, Monsieur Maillaud was downplaying the significance of the American connection. He announced that "no link is being made with the Chevaline killings" following confirmation that a heart attack was the cause of Jimmy's death.

In my interview with him, Monsieur Maillaud confirmed that is the view of the investigators, and said that they believe Iqbal probably left America because she was under extreme family pressure to do so and eventually cracked. "She might well have been happy," he said. "But the cultural pressure was too much and she couldn't live freely. It's one theory among many others."

Yet after speaking with Judy Weatherly on several occasions over the course of a month, it seems to me Iqbal and her mother Suhaila's life prior to the daughter's arrival in Britain might well justify ongoing police investigations – even if the timing of Jimmy Thompson's death is just a coincidence.

The secrets Iqbal kept so well-hidden suggest that she, or her mother, are just as plausible as primary targets for the gunman as Saad al-Hilli or the French cyclist Sylvain Mollier. We know a lot more about Saad than we do about either of the female victims. Yet Iqbal, like him, was shot by four bullets.

Chapter 14

Third theory: Sylvain Mollier

At the first chaotic press conference in Annecy, both the prosecutor and the senior police officer made it clear they were genuinely unsure whether the targets were the al-Hilli family or the French cyclist Sylvain Mollier. Either party could be "collateral damage" for the shooting of the other, they said.

Later on they muddied the waters further by implying it was possible none of the victims was a defined target. They might all have simply been in the wrong place at the wrong time when an unhinged, unfocused gunman decided to use up some bullets.

Speaking to me for this book, Monsieur Maillaud affirmed: "There are three main hypotheses, and beneath that a lot of sub-hypotheses. These are the three main theories: either the cyclist was the principal target, or the main target was the family al-Hilli or Saad al-Hilli, or the main target was no one. Logically, when we kill someone, we do so for a valid motive. Afterwards we kill the inconvenient eye-witnesses. The third of these hypotheses suggests a crazed killer, or at least someone without a motive. In this case all of them were in the wrong place at the wrong time and the killer did not want to be identified. We would be looking at them disturbing a drug deal, or a crazed man playing with his gun who decided to kill them all. For the time being, we do not have an answer. That is the problem."

Few have ever taken this "random slaughter" view seriously, and for the most part the focus has always been on Saad as the prime target.

What, however, were the plausible reasons someone might have wanted to kill the cyclist? Could it be possible Sylvain was the person the assassin had been aiming for throughout? Might a contract killer have been given a picture of this 45-year-old father, told the route he was taking on his bike that day, and given details of the best place to fire? In this scenario, the al-Hillis were a huge inconvenience to a killer who would have wanted no loose ends.

Is it possible he, or she, took the decision to do away with this troublesome family of foreigners as well so they could not provide a positive identification later on? Did Sylvain, painted as a fairly nondescript everyman with a relatively unremarkable life in a small nearby town, actually have a secret life?

This suggestion is one that is repeatedly chewed over on internet conspiracy theory chatrooms. More of these seem to validate Sylvain being the target than Saad. And from day one, prosecutor Maillaud and Lt-Col Vinnemann have offered up the cyclist-as-primary-target as a credible theory.

"Who was the target? Lt-Col Vinnemann asked rhetorically back then. "We don't know. Was it the family and was the cyclist a collateral victim? Or was it the cyclist and was the family a collateral victim? That remains to be ascertained."

Several months after the crime, information allegedly leaked from the inquiry team to the media implied that Sylvain was shot first. Having spoken to Monsieur Maillaud about this at length, however, I can reveal such a claim is impossible to verify. Simply put, no one knows who was shot first.

But in our conversation, another astonishing fact emerged: in his desperation to get away, Saad reversed over Sylvain.

The cyclist was on the ground at this stage having already been shot, said the prosecutor, and Saad might also have been shot at least once by this point.

"Two things are certain," Monsieur Maillaud told me. "Firstly, the 21 shots were fired in a very short space of time. We know they are fired while the vehicle was reversing in an arc, and we know that would be less than 60 seconds, less than a minute. The other scientific certitude that we have is that in the semi-circle movement, the al-Hillis' vehicle passed over Sylvain Mollier's body. Traces of blood were left on the car. When Sylvain Mollier fell on the ground before being run over, he had already been shot and he was bleeding; however that does not mean the shot was aimed at him. It is scientifically certain that the blood on the car was not from an injury caused by the bumper of the vehicle or the wheel of the vehicle."

It is also worth remembering that Sylvain was shot five times, one more than Saad. Two separate volleys of gunfire were aimed at him. As discussed, this might have been because he was a moving target, an unanticipated distraction for the thorough and clinical killer as he executed his victims methodically. Or it might have been because Sylvain was the intended target all along.

Indeed, the view that there was only one intended victim makes the decision to choose a weapon which can ordinarily only hold at most eight bullets at a time more rational.

The final shot into Sylvain, Monsieur Maillaud has told me, was a textbook execution. "The last shot fired at Sylvain Mollier was a bullet between the eyes," he said. "I have not said this before but it was what we call, in military terms, an execution shot."

So who was Sylvain Mollier? And who might bear a grudge against him severe enough to order his death? I visited his hometown of Ugine, about 20 minutes' drive from Chevaline, to look into it. In 15 years of working in national newspapers, I have rarely had so many doors closed in my face.

On the day he died, Sylvain was still basking in the glow of recent fatherhood. His partner Claire Schutz, scion of a well-off local family with a respected pharmacy business, had given birth to a son, Louis, in June. Louis was three months old.

Sylvain was on long-term leave from his job as a production worker at the nuclear metal factory, Cezus, at the far edge of Ugine. This wasn't just statutory paternity leave; he was taking several months, or perhaps years away from work, several people claimed at the time.

The Cezus plant is a foreboding row of warehouses and factory units tucked in beneath a steep mountain. Through metal gates, factory workers in blue uniform can be seen scuttling in and out of the drab grey buildings. Inside they make zirconium pipes for nuclear power business Areva to use in reactors. At 4pm each day the workers stream out after clocking off and disappear to a car park to head off in the direction of Ugine, a functional Alpine town with a scattering of traditional, attractive buildings disguised by ugly apartment blocks around its edge. When I visited Cezus, my inquiry at the security desk was met by a dismissive shake of the head by the female receptionist. She would not even refer my question – can anyone say anything in tribute to Sylvain Mollier – to anyone higher up.

In some newspaper articles, Sylvain has been accused of profiting from the benefits of Claire's family wealth. Claire, 16 years younger than him aged 29 at the time, was in a far better financial position than his former wife Lydie, a hairdresser who runs a salon in Ugine. Sylvain and Lydie, then 42, had divorced around six years before.

Claire's father Thierry Schutz was a self-made man, the owner with his wife Genevieve of a business in the town of Grignon called Schutz Morange Pharmacy. The Schutz family were well-connected. Genevieve is the sister of French MP Pierre Morange, a member of the centre-right UMP party, and a political party ally of former President Nicolas Sarkozy. The pharmacy company was reported to be worth more than €1million – about £0.7million. Some time after the shootings it was claimed that Claire, a trained pharmacist, had inherited the family business in its entirety.

Speaking about the handover of the pharmacy, Sylvain's brother Christophe told one journalist: "Both Claire's parents are approaching retirement and have been extremely successful and they wanted Claire to take charge. She's a qualified pharmacist and worked for them. He had been through a difficult divorce and had a lot of financial commitments so naturally was very happy with the development. However, there were serious frictions between the Molliers and Claire Schutz's family."

It was implied that Sylvain had effectively been living off his younger partner's apparent inherited wealth – sponging, to put it less delicately. One anonymous friend on the council on which her dad Thierry served for two years was reported as saying: "Sylvain came from a down-to-earth family but had growing claims on Claire's fortune. This was something Claire's family was allegedly not happy about. They were particularly concerned about Mollier's spending. There was allegedly a bitter dispute over what was going on. This swelling anger spilled out when Mollier took three years off to effectively live off Claire's money."

Friction between the Schutz family and Sylvain was said to have got so bad that they at some point cut all ties. Thierry, then 71, and Genevieve, then 68, were reported to be very unhappy this man had become financially dependant on their hard-won fortune. It was even claimed that only one of Sylvain's four siblings was invited to the funeral when Thierry took charge of the arrangements and buried Sylvain in a secret ceremony.

And it was Claire's father, Thierry Schutz, who suggested to Sylvain the fateful route up the mountain to the Le Martinet clearing, it was later reported.

Sylvain would have followed the road from Ugine towards Annecy before taking a sharp left at Chevaline to climb uphill again. A long, flat cycle path runs adjacent to the main road. In this cycling-mad country, a constant stream of bikers in their fluorescent Lycra gear and helmets pass along it all day. Sylvain was, by Brett Martin's account, an excellent cyclist. All Brett recalled was the Frenchman passing him, quickly, on the way up.

It can now be revealed, however, that Claire did not personally possess as much wealth as has been presumed. The French police have always been dismissive that these tensions could have given rise to a murder. If Sylvain was, as alleged, a male gold-digger, then it seems he could have picked a better target.

Monsieur Maillaud told me: "There has been a lot of speculation about Claire's money, but in fact she did not inherit her father's business. He has given it to her on credit, which she reimburses every month. This is a completely normal gesture on the part of a father. It is also worth remembering that Sylvain Mollier and Claire Schutz were not married, so he would not have inherited any money anyway. This just doesn't work as a theory."

Speculation that Sylvain's employment at Cezus might be relevant because of its connection to the nuclear industry has also been dismissed. True, the company is a subsidiary of the Areva nuclear group, and Sylvain worked daily with the production of zirconium pipes used in nuclear reactors. But he was almost certainly too low down the pecking order to have been in a position to pass on anything useful to someone hoping to acquire nuclear secrets, anything which would have brought him to the attention of the security services. Sylvain was a welder by trade; he was not a scientist.

As Monsieur Maillaud explained to me: "As regards the suggestion that his job in the nuclear industry might be a reason for him meeting Saad, a satellite engineer, one should remember he was a mere factory worker in a factory making pipes for Areva. The reality is less interesting than the theory. The manager of the plant has told me they produce nothing secret there, nothing out of the ordinary."

In the days after the shootings, flags flew at half-mast outside Cezus. Colleagues were offered counselling to deal with their loss and there was no suggestion Sylvain had enemies there.

In Ugine, which has a population of 7,000, Sylvain was well-liked: a rugby player whose passion for sport was only matched by his devotion to his children. Speaking the week after the massacre, Michel Chevallier, the small town's assistant mayor, commented: "Sylvain was a very reserved guy. His family was extremely important to him."

But an unnamed friend who spoke to local newspaper L'Essor Savoyard also noted that Sylvain was, where women were concerned, "a charmer". He was said to be extremely attractive to women. The friend went further, saying: "One day he confided in me that he felt he had to be careful while walking down the street because he feared he would be shot." This has so far been the only suggestion the killing might have been carried out by an angry husband, jealous that Sylvain had enjoyed a fling with his wife or partner. He sounds like a ladies' man who was well aware of his seductive capabilities. It was enough for the French authorities to add "crime passionnel" – a crime of passion – to their long list of possible motives. Monsieur Maillaud told me the possibility of a cuckolded, angry husband being the Chevaline killer is something they have examined in depth.

"Sylvain Mollier is an easier investigation for us," he explained. "He is French, his wife is French, his family is French – everything is French in regard to him. It is a lot easier. We have examined his life from every possible angle, in every aspect and we have found nothing which explains to us why anyone would want to get at this man. The only explanation is that this guy was a bit of a ladies' man, and someone might have been angry with him for this. If we look at the last two years of his life, he lived with Claire Schutz and he had a child. Clearly he was someone who enjoyed chatting up women, but there were not different women in his bed every night. That is simply not true. He was no Casanova. What we would be looking at is a situation in which he seduced a friend's girlfriend two years beforehand, and then two years later this guy goes there to shoot him and finds himself confronted by the al-Hilli family. We are then looking at someone very well acquainted with using a gun and capable of killing a whole family, including a child. Everything is possible, but that cannot be our first hypothesis."

Very few people in Ugine have spoken about Sylvain Mollier, but those who have seem confident in stating he was simply a man in the wrong place at the wrong time.

Speaking two months on from the massacre, his retired aunt Suzanne Ginolin dismissed the apparently speculative theories as "nonsense".

"He was just a very straightforward, quiet-living

man," Madame Ginolin told the Daily Telegraph. "He had no enemies; he was very friendly and charming. There's no way that he was the cause of all this."

His cousin Alain Mollier-Camus was quoted as saying: "He was a sportsman and a family man. There's nothing hidden there."

Since the murders, neither the Schutz family members nor Lydie, now remarried with the surname Ringot, have wanted to speak about whether Sylvain might have been the real target. His father Roger died in 2011 aged 78. His mother, Suzanne, had been in a care home since long before her son's death. She was reportedly only vaguely aware of what had happened to Sylvain, one of her four sons.

Lydie has two teenage sons from her marriage to him, Mathis and Leo. She is an active member of her local community, volunteering as secretary for a local business association. Although their split has been described as acrimonious, her ex-husband's departure has surely left her and their two sons deeply upset.

From the outset Sylvain's family and friends have insisted on absolute privacy. They have resisted all interview requests. No one other than those intimately connected to him were invited to the memorial service in his hometown of Ugine. A wall of silence has enclosed the whole community. When I went there, everyone I approached seized up at the mention of the story. I visited the home of his brother Francois and the door was slammed shut the second after I mentioned Sylvain's name. It was the same at other relatives' homes.

I called his brother Christophe, hoping he would be able to expand on his earlier comments. He said: "I have nothing to say on this subject. It went badly for me after I spoke to a British journalist before. I don't know anyone who would like to talk. It is still very raw; not much time has passed."

In Britain one would expect many column inches to be filled with tributes to someone killed in such a callous fashion. But in France it is quite common for someone so dramatically murdered to be remembered much more privately.

Local journalist Jean-Francois Casanova told me the Mollier family and his employers have hired a lawyer to monitor French and international media. He claimed they "go on the attack" against any journalist who speculates on why Mollier was at Le Martinet that day. "The company has paid for the lawyer," Monsieur Casanova told me.

"They are working alongside the family to ensure nothing derogatory is said about Sylvain. The local newspaper even received a legal letter simply for covering a service in his honour, saying it was a breach of his private life. His siblings, his in-laws and his employers have all shut down. It is difficult to understand why. To everyone here, it seems so implausible that he could have been the target. He was not an intellectual scientist with access to nuclear secrets; he was a factory worker."

Monsieur Maillaud and the investigators do not regard this as at all suspicious.

"The family are very private, but every time we have asked them a question they have tried to find the answer," he told me.

Court documents from October 2011 confirm the handover of the Schutz-Morange Pharmacy, in Grignon. Sylvain and Claire had been living together for around a year by this time and Claire would have been pregnant with Louis, yet she describes herself as a "a spinster not signed up to a civil partnership".

Just before his death, Sylvain had also won the legal right to take three years off from the factory where he worked. He was not only looking after Louis, but also his two teenage sons from his first marriage.

What is also undoubtedly true is that Sylvain was riding a new £4,000 racing bike on the day he was murdered. Although he was a keen cyclist, this does seem a lot for someone on a fairly average wage to have spent on a bike.

Any question marks over Sylvain are though, it seems, about minor issues, and the investigators insist they have less reason to believe Sylvain was the target than the al-Hillis.

"We have found nothing around this that is a credible motive for shooting him dead," Monsieur Maillaud said. He added that taking all the evidence into account, "the theory of Sylvian Mollier being the target" had to go "at the bottom of the pile".

Chapter 15

Fourth theory: a lone madman or a racist killer

There are plenty of aspects to the Annecy slaughter which give credence to the less scrutinised theory of a lone madman being responsible, a psychopath on the loose.

The antique semi-automatic pistol, for example, might not be exactly the first choice of a modern, professional assassin.

The location is an ideal spot for someone to lurk in wait in confidence that people will pass alone at some point in the day.

Also, there are the loose ends: the killer was undoubtedly ruthless but, unlike Matt Damon's CIA covert assassin Jason Bourne, not so efficiently trained as to leave behind no witnesses at all.

It could all point to someone deranged, someone in the grip of an insane bloodlust from which he later awakened and returned to a normal life; a psychopath able to do something truly appalling and then live with his dark secret without letting anyone know.

The lone madman line was one prosecutor Maillaud talked up in the plodding early months of his mammoth investigation. From a police perspective it would certainly make for a much simpler investigation if the whole thing could be pinned on an unstable local individual.

A line of inquiry is known as a "piste" in France, like a ski route. There have now been so many in the Annecy probe that the crime-board must resemble a map of a Trois Vallées resort, with countless twisting, interlocking runs flowing down to nowhere.

"The hypothesis of a lone and psychologically disturbed killer, is gaining ground," Monsieur Maillaud said to French newspaper Le Monde in late October 2012. He and his team were coming round to the view that this profile of the killer fitted better than that of a professional hired assassin. The theory was said to be pushing aside the hitherto preferred view that a family feud explained the killings. This contradicted initial suggestions that detectives were hunting a hitman able to commit an act of "gross savagery"and then flee the scene without leaving a trace.

An unnamed source told the respected Paris-based title that detectives were increasingly exploring "the possibility of a lone and psychologically disturbed killer".

"They have carried out checks at all psychiatric hospitals in the region and are tracking down all patients who may have been recently released or were on day release," the inquiry insider was quoted as saying. "They are especially focusing on those with previous convictions for gun violence or who were known to be attracted to firearms. Investigators are on this basis also contacting gun clubs and hunting clubs in the region. But so far they have had no satisfactory results to their inquiries."

Commentators pointed to France's more relaxed gun laws as a simple explanation for how someone could be so unhinged they could carry out a mass murder but not beforehand come to the attention of law-enforcement authorities.

France has one of the highest levels of civilian gun ownership in Europe. Handguns, semi-automatic weapons and pump-action shotguns are legal if held by active gun club members. Owners must have a licence for such weapons and undergo a medical check. Bolt-action rifles and semi-automatic guns limited to three-rounds can be acquired with either a sports shooting licence or a hunting licence. In this instance, only local police would need to be informed.

Fully-automatic firearms are banned in France, although recent events prove weapons are being easily smuggled into the country. The most striking example of this is the terrorist atrocity in Paris in January 2015. Charlie Hebdo killers Cherif and Said Kouachi, together with kosher grocery jihadist Amedy Coulibaly had between them amassed an arsenal worth a total of more than £19,000.

In January 2013, the lone psychopath theory had resurfaced when detectives suggested the al-Hilli murder could be connected to a shooting in Switzerland. Ex-soldier Florian Berthouzoz, 33, had shot dead three women and wounded two men in the village of Daillon, near Geneva in January that year. French police made a formal request to interview Berthouzoz, who had been kicked out of the Swiss Army for threatening people with guns. In 2005 he had had weapons confiscated because of his mental state.

Daillon is only 100 miles from Lake Annecy, so the reasons for the detectives' interest were obvious. Berthouzoz, a psychiatric patient with drug problems, began his spree by storming out of a restaurantand picking up his army rifle and a hunting gun at his flat. He fired shots indiscriminately from his home before prowling a multi-storey car park. His female victims were aged 32, 54, and 79. The men, aged 33 and 63, were badly wounded. Local police eventually cornered him and shot him in the shoulder.

In Berthouzoz police had identified a man with no compunction about killing and with no obvious signs of remorse for his actions – a man disturbed enough to slaughter a family of total strangers and a passer-by. He fitted one of the profiles put out by Monsieur Maillaud in one of his many briefings: "We are looking for unbalanced people, capable of extreme violence; people who have access to weapons – hunters, collectors, shooting club members, some with psychiatric problems."

It was always highly possible that the answers investigators were looking for lay somewhere in Switzerland, where about a quarter of the nation's population of eight million people own guns. In Switzerland, army-issue weapons like the Luger P06 account for the deaths of more than 300 people every year.

But a few days later the possible link between Berthouzoz and Chevaline had been ruled out. The mentally-ill killer was nowhere near Annecy on September 5, 2012. His victims in Daillon were all women whom he knew. He was taking revenge for some perceived slight.

Then, in February 2014, a 48-year-old former police officer called Eric Devouassoux was arrested at his home in Talloires, a Lake Annecy village a few miles from Chevaline. With a goatee beard like the one on the mystery motorcyclist e-fit and very similar facial features, it was easy to see why investigators had made the connection. Devouassoux hoarded Second World War weapons at his home. He had been a reservist in the French military, receiving combat training, and had been attached to the Gendarmerie Nationale, a branch of the Armed Forces, since 2001.

What is more, married father-of-three Devouassoux seemingly had a grudge to bear. Although he was still a serving officer at the time of the murders, he was fired from his job in June 2013 after being the community officer for 15 years in another local village, Menthon-Saint-Bernard. There, locals said, his main role was helping children across the road and stopping cars parking in undesignated bays. It was claimed at the time he had been caught siphoning petrol from his police patrol car. There are suggestions an investigation into his alleged misconduct was taking place at the time of the killings in September 2012.

Outside his home police found an old grey and black motorbike covered with a yellow tarpaulin and took it away for forensic tests. In searches of the Talloires property and a house owned by his wife's parents detectives also discovered 7.65mm ammunition, like that used in a Luger P06, and a user's manual of the P06. The total haul included around 40 guns, grenades and a mortar shell.

Prosecutor Maillaud added fuel to the fire when he said of Devouassoux: "He doesn't like foreigners – but he doesn't really like anyone who is not from here.

"It's certain that the profile of this man whose interest in weapons, his passion for the Luger, have made him an interesting target as far as the investigators are concerned so we will carry on digging."

A friend of Devouassoux, Jean-Luc Falcy, was

arrested at the same time. He reportedly tried to flee when heavily-armed officers from the GIGN, a tactical military unit, turned up at his home. Here they found ammunition, explosives and detonators.

It all sounded so damning.

Devouassoux and Falcy were questioned by police for four days at the headquarters in Chambéry.

But after DNA tests and further searches, the two men were released. Detectives could not make a substantial link between Devouassoux and the deaths of the al-Hilli family and Sylvain Mollier. All the connections between this local man and the area's worst-ever crime were circumstantial. The fact that Devouassoux's phone signal put him in the general area of the murders at the time was insufficient as he lived close by anyway. The Luger handgun found in one of the searches was not an exact match for the pistol used in the attack. The motorbike and his crash helmet did not match those described by the forestry worker. One villager in Menthon-Saint-Bernard said Devouassoux was "too stupid" to be the cold-blooded assassin most believe to be responsible for the killings.

Devouassoux was an eccentric, occasionally irate, occasionally racist gun obsessive, but not a murderer, police concluded.

The friends were, however, charged in relation to illegal arms trafficking, charges which remained outstanding as this book was being written.

Security guard Devouassoux complained in an interview with French news network BFMTV that his life had been ruined by his arrest and public exposure. He said he had lost his livelihood, his reputation and his belongings because of the investigation. He even wrote to French President Francois Hollande to demand an explanation for his alleged mistreatment.

"I was pillaged by the police when I was arrested," Devouassoux wrote in his letter to the Élysée Palace. "They have still not returned three computers, including those belonging to my wife and my son, a motorbike, a scooter and hunting rifles. I was a security guard in Switzerland and my employer is ready to take me back. But under the terms of my bail, I am banned from going to Switzerland."

Since the letter was sent in May 2014 there has been no further action against him in relation the murders. It would seem his fetish for old guns, his proximity to the murder scene, and his alleged grudge against foreigners were all a series of coincidences.

After such high drama, and finally a sniff of a real

lead, the investigators had to go back to the drawing board.

If nothing else, the arrests of Devouassoux and Falcy provided an insight into how easy it would be for local eccentrics to build up a substantial armoury without coming to the police's attention. Devouassoux collected guns just like the one used to kill the al-Hillis and Sylvain Mollier, and it seems that prior to his arrest none of his former police colleagues had been aware of his obsession.

As the Charlie Hebdo attacks in Paris have demonstrated, France is a country with deep-seated tensions between its Muslim, Jewish and Christian communities. It is not only in the capital where young Muslim people feel abandoned by the state and are attracted towards the extremist ideologies of ISIS and al-Qaeda. Earlier in 2012, an Islamist attack took place in Toulouse. Mohamed Merah went on three killing sprees, gunning down seven people including two young children, a rabbi and two French paratroopers, at point-blank range. Police eventually shot him dead at his flat in the southern city on March 22 after a 32-hour siege. As was the case with Coulibaly in Paris, Merah claimed to be taking revenge for France's involvement in foreign conflicts in Muslim nations. In his case it was Afghanistan; in that of Coulibaly and the Kouachi brothers it was the bombing sorties against ISIS in Syria.

The tensions have been successfully exploited by the far-right in France. The Front National party, led by Marine Le Pen, is firmly established as the third largest political force in France. In 2002 Marine's father Jean-Marie Le Pen managed to get through to the presidential run-offs and finish second to Jacques Chirac.

Against this background, a lone killer targeting Saad and his family might have been motivated by religious and racial hatred. He might have seen this family of Iraqi origin in the Lake Annecy area in the preceding days and decided to vent his hatred for all Muslims against them. Such a deluded, ill-informed person might see their deaths as justified in the wake of Merah's Toulouse atrocities. The killings, if carried out by such a person, would have been motivated by cold-blooded revenge, a distorted way of settling the scores on behalf of France's white majority.

Another seemingly plausible explanation for the killing is that it was one of a recent spate of attacks by gangs on groups of tourists across France. In the preceding months there had been a series of hold-ups involving masked attackers within about 50 miles of the crime scene. Thieves typically tricked their victims by faking accidents or pretending to need help. One gang reportedly tried to steal a Ford Fiesta and a Peugeot.

Earlier in 2012 the British Foreign Office had warned tourists about an emerging "pattern of incidents" in the Alps and south-eastern France. These incidents related to gangs targeting foreign-registered cars on motorways.

Edmund King, president of the AA, described these gangs of marauding robbers as "bandits". He went on: "There have been incidents in the south of France and in places around Lyon. They look for UK-registered cars then they flash their lights and perhaps point at the tourist car's wheels. The tourists stop and, while one gang member distracts them, another steals from their car. French police have been cracking down on these gangs but there have been isolated and organised incidents from particular gangs in particular areas."

There was, however, one major flaw in this line of enquiry. Whoever killed the al-Hilli family and Sylvain Mollier had stolen nothing. The victims still had their wallets, their camera, their mobile phones and their passports when their bodies were found. It seems almost certain the assassin who murdered four people beyond Chevaline was no ordinary robber. If he was, he came away empty-handed and created an awful lot of unhelpful police attention for his criminal network. It would have been among the most botched robberies in recent history.

Detectives did briefly check out potential links to car-jackings that happened 50 miles away on the same day. Masked bandits tried to steal a Ford Fiesta at Isère a few hours after the murder and at 1am the same gang tried to steal a Peugeot 205 in nearby Ville-sous-Anjou. There was found to be no connection.

Several murders in France with similar facets to the Annecy killings have also raised interest. In November 2012, 29-year-old Belgian Xavier Baligant was shot four times at a rest area near Nancy in eastern France while he was heading home following a camping trip. His two sons Jordan, seven, and Dylan, five, were sleeping in the car but escaped unharmed. What was striking about this case was that police believed the gun used was very similar to the Swiss army pistol used at the Le Martinet clearing. Again, however, no substantial connection between the two murders of foreign tourists on camping trips was made by the detective team.

Exactly one year later, in November 2013, masked gunmen shot dead a woman in the village of Lathuile, a few miles from Chevaline on the opposite bank of the lake. Two men wearing waterproof jackets and gloves broke into the home of the owners of a private camping site. At 2am they attacked the woman and her husband who managed the "Ideal" holiday resort, another popular haunt for British holidaymakers. The woman was killed by a bullet to the chest. Her husband was hit with the butt of the weapon.

Another arbitrary slaying in a peaceful beauty spot. Lake Annecy starts to seem like the murder capital of France when these killings are collected together. It is, however, a place with a very low crime rate and this murder was also nothing to do with the al-Hilli shooting.

In late 2014 a hunter was arrested after a French building contractor was found dead with a bullet in his head on an isolated country road 50 miles from Chevaline. Jean-Francois Hauteville, 47, suffered close-range bullet wounds to the head as he sat in his Peugeot Boxer van in a wooded area near Neuvecelle, close to Lake Geneva. The vehicle's engine was still running when a passer-by found his body slumped behind the steering wheel, with the driver's window open.

A few days after this happened, a fellow gun enthusiast was placed under investigation. The parallels with the Chevaline massacre were self-evident, but this too was completely unrelated. These various totally unconnected crimes received far more coverage in the UK than they would normally have because of the initial links made to what had happened in September 2012. Every news story published since the shootings has left a soiled footprint on the serene postcard image of Lake Annecy. Just as Praia de Luz is now associated with the disappearance of Madeleine McCann for a whole generation of British tourists, Lake Annecy is associated with the murders of the al-Hilli family.

The other motive that was touted in the opening days of the inquiry was that the al-Hilli family – and cyclist Sylvain Mollier – had disturbed a drug deal. This would suggest a mystery motorcyclist and the mystery 4x4 driver were up at the remote parking spot doing a handover when they were suddenly surprised by a large group of people. Needless to say, this explanation has never really been seriously considered, especially since the motorcyclist has been discounted. Chevaline residents say they have never heard of dealing taking place up the Combe d'Ire road.

Their idyllic village, they said, suffered no problems like that.

Chapter 16

A hitman for hire: £405 for each victim

At a one-year-on news conference, prosecutor Eric Maillaud said: "He [the murderer] needed time to change the magazine. The only logical conclusion is that we are dealing with a very experienced gunman."

The Annecy prosecutor refuses to use the term "professional", believing it credits inhumane killers with a respectable career. But he was happy to describe the suspect as "hardened" and "experienced in situations of stress".

"All we know is that there was one killer and he knew what he was doing; he was able to hit a moving target and change magazines," he candidly admitted, adding, "we have no idea of his exact profile".

As has been the case throughout the joint Franco-British inquiry, the Surrey Police team said very little.

For many, the hypothesis of a psychotic gun obsessive being the perpetrator was a non-starter from the outset, and in June 2013 Monsieur Maillaud openly discussed what most people watching developments already believed.

Interviewed for a TV documentary, Monsieur Maillaud entertained the notion the culprit was probably a hired contract killer from abroad who would have most likely picked up the gun locally. "It is only in the films that a contract killer comes from Australia or China with a plastic weapon hidden in a tube of toothpaste and risks going through all the airport security checks," he said in a telling yet typically colourful and off-the-cuff sound-bite.

He continued: "Is it too far-fetched to suppose that a hit-man, a contract killer trying to kill a whole family, would source a firearm locally? Of course not: so it doesn't mean that because a firearm is sourced locally the killer is also local."

It made sense. An assassin coming from abroad would far rather use something sourced locally than have to transport their own arsenal. They would only need a little time to test the weapon before being able to carry out their paymaster's instructions. This also implies the assassin might have been connected to a network capable of finding local suppliers for semi-automatic pistols.

Around this time in the investigation details of two potential hitmen started to emerge. Two contrasting stories leaked out from the inquiry team, one apparently originating in France and the other in Britain.

One claim was that an Iraqi who was living in Belgium but had served time in France had been offered €100,000, about £81,000, to "eliminate an Iraqi settled in England". The ex-convict was wire-tapped "following a specific claim from another prisoner that he could have been involved in a contract to kill Iraqis," said Monsieur Maillaud. The detectives looked into the unnamed man's background for more than 18 months and arrested him in June 2014 when he visited northern France.

The 35-year-old was interrogated for three days and held in custody in the northern city of Lille. But in that time he provided a convincing alibi and was cleared of any involvement in the shootings. He had not in fact been approached, investigators concluded. Monsieur Maillaud confirmed: "He denied any involvement in a contract whatsoever, and we could not establish a link with the al-Hilli family."

The man was subsequently jailed for unrelated offences but here was yet another hopeful lead that ultimately went nowhere.

Separately it was suggested that an "English witness" had put forward a claim that the al-Hillis were assassinated by a mercenary from the Balkans. This time the fee was said to be €2,000, around £1,620 – or just or just £405 per victim.

The Balkan connection made sense. Expert contract killers are highly likely to be from the former Yugoslavia or Albania where there remains a ready supply of people in need of hard cash who learned deadly skills during the Bosnia and Kosovo conflicts. The travelling distance by road from Serbia to Annecy via Croatia, Slovenia and northern Italy is only 12 hours. By the time police had time to respond to the massacre, a hitman could have already changed vehicle at least once and been well on his way back to obscurity in the Balkans.

Hiring a contract killer - a mercenary well-practised in assassinating a human being and then slipping back into normal life without raising alarm - sounds like a transaction that could only take place in a movie. The anti-hero of the French film Léon, directed by Luc Besson, is the kind of figure most people would conjure up. In that acclaimed movie, the lead character only ever receives minimal information from his employers. He keeps himself in extraordinary physical shape with a daily exercise routine and a strict diet. He keeps his guns well-oiled and always has a plentiful stock of ammunition. He does a job, and then disappears to his nondescript apartment in Paris, where few ever take notice because he rarely says or does anything noteworthy. He is the kind of man who would be able carry out an assignment without flinching.

Leon is a fictional character, but recent evidence suggests hiring a contract killer in Europe is almost as straight-forward as the movie portrayal.

Vice.com reported in 2013 how websites in the Czech Republic and other Eastern European nations were openly offering hitmen for hire. On one site, said to be running since February 2013, costs began at $350 (£240) for a "light shake-down" and went up to a range of options for an arranged murder. These included death from natural causes or an "accident", a random murder in a fight or a "classic" ordered hit. Customised extras included leaving the target naked in a forest.

This was not thought to be a hoax site and politicians in Russia took it seriously enough to make repeated calls for it to be blacklisted. The hitmen advertised were thought to be Soviet Army veterans who fought the mujahideen in Afghanistan and professional boxers and wrestlers who lost their livelihood when the Iron Curtain fell.

In January 2014 a study by criminologists at Birmingham City University found 27 cases of contract killing in Britain between 1974 and 2013. These were committed by 36 men, including accomplices, and one woman. They found the average cost of a hit was £15,180, with prices paid ranging from £200 to £100,000. Most involved a gun, with three victims stabbed, five beaten to death and two strangled.

Using off-the-record interviews with informants, interviews with offenders and former offenders, court transcripts and newspaper archives, the academics identified patterns of hitman behaviour. What struck them was that the transaction between a contract killer and his employer was often very dull. Rather than being a shady deal carried out in a back room, the meetings often happened in public and in broad daylight. They discovered killers typically carried out the murder on a street close to the their target's home. A significant proportion got cold feet or bungled the job.

I wondered if the study's lead author Professor

David Wilson, a regular advisor to the police on cases including the Suffolk Strangler, could shed any light on the Annecy killings.

Professor Wilson and his team did not include the al-Hilli case in their final published paper as it happened outside the UK but they did look at it. He told me his firm belief is that the perpetrator of the al-Hilli murders was among the most highly trained hitmen, a man who would be identified as a "master" hitman in the categories identified in the academic paper. At the top of a notional career ladder that begins with novice killers, master hitmen are described as being so "adept" that the deaths of their victims often do "not even raise suspicion".

He said: "We would theorise that the person who committed the hit was a master hitman, somebody who corresponded with that profile. The master hitman is never caught. You only see the evidence of their hit. Often they would do things like leave bullets or leave the gun because those bullets or bullet casings or that gun would never be connected back to them. There were a number of things that led us to this conclusion. There were also a number of things that were very unusual and very atypical. What was typical of a master hitman at work was that the hit itself seemed to be quite carefully co-ordinated.

I know people will say it wasn't, and that it was accidental, but actually when you look at a number of hits that have taken place in Britain often there is quite a complicated narrative to getting the victim of the hit in the place that the hitman wants him to be at."

Professor Wilson says the closest comparison to the al-Hilli case in Britain is with the murder of gangland boss Frank McPhee in the Glasgow area of Maryhill in 2000. McPhee was killed by a single shot to the head only 500 metres from a police station by an assassin armed with a rifle fitted with a telescopic sight. The murderer has never been brought to justice. It is widely thought that McPhee was chased by one hitman so he would unknowingly walk into the sights of the highly trained sniper who fired the fatal shot.

"It's quite clear in that case the target was chased away from an allotment to get him to the site where the hitman was waiting for him," he explained. "The hit on Frank McPhee was the most professional hit ever to take place on the British mainland. Frank McPhee was chased from one part of Glasgow back to his doorstep where the contract killer had him in his sights."

He added that the supposedly messier aspects of the Annecy killings should surprise no one.

"Lots of people misinterpreted elements of the al-Hilli hit; for example, there were witnesses. But actually this misinterpretation is part of the fantasy in which hits take place in the underworld, in smoky bars and in casinos, well hidden from members of the public.

"Actually most British hits that we studied often had people that were witnesses to the hit, who looked upon the hit in abject horror. They were more usually carried out in the open, on pavements, sometimes as the target was out walking their dog, or going shopping, with passers-by watching on in horror. People couldn't believe what they were witnessing and often couldn't describe the person who did the hit because they were so scared afterwards."

Professor Wilson contends the fact that there were several victims might have surprised the killer too.

"Often the hit will only be about one person," the professor said. "It is very unusual that this case involves a group of people. The contract is typically about hitting a particular person at a particular time. With the al-Hilli family we are dealing with a family; it's atypical in terms of the numbers. But why should we presume that the contract killer actually knew there would be the number of people actually going to that particular spot where he was going to encounter the al-Hillis? We are making a presumption that the hitman didn't think it was just going to be the father that turned up. The fact that the entire family went with him may not have been calculated. The little girl being shielded from her mother might seem unusual, but to me and my colleagues at the criminology department here at Birmingham City University it didn't seem so at all. What is surprising therefore is him overcoming that disadvantage to be able to still commit the hit. At the end of the day this has been someone who has been rather successful if you think about it in that way. There is no local intelligence apart from rumours."

He also agrees with Monsieur Maillaud that the killer is likely not from the area.

"Often the reason why you don't catch a master hitman is that he doesn't come from the local community, but enters the local community, makes the hit, and then exits from the local community. The hit has to be done with some speed. You have to get in, commit the hit and leave.

"This is why often hitmen are caught. Often if it's not a master hitman when there is local intelligence about the person who may have committed the hit. I know there have been suspects in the French community, but those don't seem to have led anywhere."

Professor Wilson's most likely scenario is that Saad was duped by the assassin into travelling up to the remote lay-by. Le Martinet, he points out, normally attracts only hardy cyclists and walkers.

"There didn't seem to be any particular local reasons why they would go there. It didn't seem to be a particularly outstanding beauty spot that people in that particular area would want to go to. It did seem to be a constructed meeting. That would fit the pattern associated with master hitmen.

"It seems to me that he was lured there. That was always where the hit was going to take place. Whether the contract killer knew he was going to turn up with all his family seems to be speculation.

"If we look at the dynamics of the hit this seems to me rather well professionally thought-through when we look at the other hits. With one exception only, the hitmen that I have studied, none of them are psychopathic. These are people who accept a contract. They are extrinsically motivated because they want to make money. They often come from a background or have used firearms regularly. The motivation is not at all personal. When we talk about psychopathic behaviour we are talking about people who are motivated intrinsically. I don't think this could be a psychopath who just happened to be there at that particular time and only targeted those particular people. Why didn't he also target the British cyclist?"

Professor Wilson also agrees with prosecutor Maillaud and other experts about the use of the fairly antiquated Luger P06 semi-automatic pistol not contradicting the hitman theory.

"The gun here is fairly typical. Any gun that can fire a bullet is going to achieve the objective and that is to kill the target. As long as it fires, the contract killer is happy. In the case of Frank McPhee the gun was left at the site of the murder. As long as they are forensically aware the gun is irrelevant. It is never going to be connected to the person who committed the hit."

Professor Wilson draws an analogy with the gun that was used to kill Jill Dando in 1999 which was a workshop conversion of a replica or decommissioned gun. For many years this was put forward as proof that the murder could not be the work of a professional assassin. But in the cold case review following the acquittal of Barry George it was concluded that the BBC Crimewatch presenter was indeed shot dead by a professional assassin.

Chapter 17

Fifth theory: a Mossad assassination

So if the Annecy massacre was the work of a professional killer, for whom were they working? For many, the notion of a private individual with a personal score to settle is not a satisfactory explanation. Certainly on the internet talk of conspiracy is rife with allegations especially that the Israeli security service Mossad killed Saad because of his political views and the possibility that he acted on these somehow through his job in satellite technology.

Of course, blaming Israel is something of knee-jerk response online to any and all unexplained events. The motivation for this is often at best idiocy and at worst anti-semitism. But enough of Saad's close friends have given at least mild credence to the possibility to make it worth examining in a little more detail.

Shia Muslim Saad made no secret of his hatred of Israel. His politics and his opinion of what was going on in the Middle East especially were based on voracious online reading. He knew details of Israeli attacks on the Gaza Strip, and had closely followed the 2006 Israel-Hezbollah War in which more than 1,000 Lebanese citizens were killed, as well as hundreds of Israelis.

A Skype Messenger conversation between Saad and his close friend James Mathews in February 2011 provides an insight into his provocative and at times unpalatable stance. Commenting on the Tahrir Square uprising the day Egyptian leader Hosni Mubarak was toppled, he says "the Jews and their lobbies" have been causing problems in the aftermath of the revolution. James asks "what now", to which Saad replies: "Let's hope they rip up the treaty with Israel."

Saad also chatted regularly on Skype with Gary Aked. Not long before his death Saad had changed his profile picture on the messaging service from a photo of his eldest daughter Zainab to an image of a bearded Arabic leader. In April 2012 he had posted a web link to an interview conducted by Wikileaks founder Julian Assange with Hassan

Nasrallah, leader of militant Islamist group Hezbollah.

"Saad didn't have a problem with Jews generally, just those in Israel," Gary claimed to the Sunday Mirror. "He read the Koran and it was always left open in the front living room of the house. He was guarded about who he spoke to about his beliefs, but he did confide in me."

Gary told me: "Saad would often be chatting online to people abroad. He'd be chatting in Arabic. He was quite vocal. This was the only thing that concerned me. He didn't like the Jews in Israel, although he didn't mind Jews as people. To him, Israel should still be Palestine, Arab territory. He thought the Jews nicked it. We had some long discussions about this, which got very heated. I was Christian he was Muslim and we would have these chats about Abraham being the father of both Jews and Muslims. But he was on these chat pages talking about how bad it was that the Jews were running the world and that people didn't know about it.

"He really believed they were taking over everything. Saad believed 9/11 was organised by the Jews to get the Americans to fight against the Arabs. He thought it was done just to start that war in Iraq. He got very heated about it. I said, 'That's crazy to believe the Jews could have instigated that to cause this war. That's madness.' But he was adamant.

"I had warned him. I'd ask what he was doing it for. I remember him saying to me he was chatting to someone in Iraq while he was talking to me in the room at the time. On one occasion he loaned me this book about atrocities in Iraq and Iran. It was about how America and England do these things that we don't hear about. He told me was really angry about all of this and he wanted to do something about it. I told him not to. I thought that after he had the kids he was a lot less heated."

It is the firmness of Saad's convictions that has fuelled speculation he might have accessed sensitive technology secrets to sell to Israeli enemy states like Iran, or to Hezbollah. This relates back to his work for SSTL in Surrey, and his involvement in other hi-tech projects through which he might supposedly have gleaned sensitive information of value to those causes he backed.

Among those who believe that this could be a credible explanation for the murders are his cousin Hussain al-Hilli in Baghdad. Speaking to the Daily Telegraph four months after the massacre, he said: "We used to discuss politics in our online conversations, and I was surprised by how radical he was. He was very supportive of Palestine, Hezbollah and Iran. If he tried to give his technology to one of those Middle Eastern powers, he would incur the anger of their rivals. I have no proof of this, but if he was stuck between them, there could be some consequences."

Hussain contends that this tendency of Saad's not to hide his views and his career could have brought him to the attention of Mossad and that Mossad would not hesitate to wipe out someone offering trade secrets to Iran.

Saad posted his views at home using several of the expensive computers he had set up himself. It certainly would not have been difficult for Mossad agents to trace his IP address and identify him. Its assassinations are known to be clinical, swiftly executed and rarely leave any evidence behind. Could there be any significant parallels between the al-Hilli murders and known Mossad hits?

The assassination of Canadian scientist Gerald Bull – like Saad an engineer – in Brussels in 1990 stands out. Bull's main professional achievement was in the development of long-range artillery and he achieved considerable notoriety with the course of his career. After working in his native Canada for many years, Bull was imprisoned and sued in the US for selling weapons to South Africa under Apartheid. For several years before his death, Bull, 62, had been involved in a quest to launch a satellite into orbit using a huge artillery piece. His particular focus was Project Babylon, working for the Iraqi Government to build a super-gun. He reportedly engaged the interest of Saddam Hussein himself when he offered to design and create a 150m-long cannon capable of such launches. It was supposed to send a 2,000kg projectile into orbit.

Simultaneously, as part of the financing deal, Bull agreed to work on the Scud missile project for Saddam. He had made calculations for the new nose-cone needed for the higher re-entry speeds and temperatures the Scud missile would face. This was clearly something that alarmed Israel, which would, in later years, be targeted by those Iraqi Scuds.

Bull's apartment suffered several break-ins, in which nothing was taken, seemingly threats from his enemies. Then, still in pursuit of the project, he was shot five times in the head at point-blank range by suspected Mossad agents in March 1990.

There is no doubt this killing bears some

resemblances to that of Saad al-Hilli, with four shots at extremely close range through a car window.

But the differences are many. Saad's wife and mother-in-law were also killed, as well as the cyclist Sylvain. Besides, Bull was clearly thought a threat to the security of Israel.

Other suspected Mossad operations on foreign soil could also be considered. The Mossad targets in each case are engineers, scientists or enemy agents engaged in acquiring technical details for weapons development.

In February 2011 Palestinian engineer Dirar Abu Sisi vanished from a train en route to the Ukranian capital Kiev from Kharkiv. He had been planning to apply for Ukrainian citizenship. Three weeks later he reappeared in an Israeli jail.

In the late 1990s Mossad was tipped off that two Iranian agents were in Johannesburg thought to be on a mission to procure advanced weapons systems from the state-owned defence company. Posing as South African intelligence, Israeli agents abducted the Iranians, drove them to a warehouse, and beat and intimidated them before forcing them to leave the country.

The most public alleged Mossad hit in recent times was the killing of a Hamas commander in his hotel room in Dubai in 2010. In all, 26 suspected Mossad agents are thought to have travelled to the country on bogus passports for the operation. The operatives entered the Hamas commander's room and allegedly tortured and interrogated him before carrying out the murder. Their bogus papers apparently included six British passports cloned from those of real British nationals living in Israel. Dubai's police chief has said he is "completely sure that it was Mossad". No one has ever been brought to justice.

As for the murders at Le Martinet, however, it is hard to form a convincing argument that is was the work of the Israeli secret service. Is it really plausible that a Mossad agent might have bought a local Luger that jammed or ran out of bullets? There is no evidence that Saad even wanted to find and sell secrets to Israel's enemies, and he could not have done so because he did not have access.

And surely being a late-night chatroom ranter is not enough to trigger a Mossad hit? On any given evening there must be thousands of those around the world espousing similar views.

Gary Aked said: "When he got shot in France, my first reaction was, 'Flipping heck, what's he been saying!' If this was a hit I couldn't think of anything else that would have caused a problem.

I thought he had maybe upset someone on one of the chatrooms. All these people on the radio were saying it was a hit. I thought, 'A hit, on Saad and Iqbal, that's crazy! That's not possible.'"

Even Gary said at the time to the Sunday Mirror: "I think it's possible he has offended someone and Mossad has taken offence and put a hit out on him."

But these days his views are different. Although he thinks it conceivable that security agencies might have been aware of Saad's online conversations, he finds it absurd to believe Mossad ordered the hit. Gary, like many others, believes the notion the cyclist Sylvain Mollier was the target is much more plausible.

Gary insisted Saad was no terrorist and would never have converted his anger into violent actions, or assisted those who might have been preparing terrorist acts against Israel. He described Saad as a man of "words and beliefs".

Gary told me: "I would rule out work. He wasn't into anything nuclear; he wasn't into any defence contracts. He wouldn't have got the clearance for sensitive defence contracts because of his Iraq background. It was definitely not the cause of his death."

Chapter 18

Sixth theory: industrial espionage

Does Saad's work hold any clues? The police have certainly not abandoned his hi-tech profession as a worthwhile line of enquiry. During our lengthy interview in his office, prosecutor Eric Maillaud repeatedly returned to the theme. He revealed Saad had some sensitive information which he had acquired from SSTL on his own personal computers. He was, the prosecutor claimed, probably breaching a clause in his contract. What the investigators have been unable to establish is whether this has any relevance to their murder inquiry.

"A theory that is too tough to dig into is the possibility of industrial espionage," Monsieur Maillaud told me. "It is true that Saad al-Hilli had in his computers material coming from his workplace that he should not have had. But at the same time, as his employer tells us, he was a respected engineer with a very good reputation and CV, and he was a real enthusiast, someone who loved to amass information. The fact that something was forbidden does not mean he didn't want that information for himself. What I am talking about here are other satellites and programmes for the design of satellites which his company was working on and which were covered by confidentiality, about which he shouldn't normally have had access. It's sure that this satellite theory had interested, and still does interest, the investigators. That company sells satellites, and while we know these are not military satellites, it's obvious that a meteorological or agricultural satellite can be transformed for other uses. It would not be the first or the last time. And here there is a problem: if we want to properly investigate this the company will not help us. We have no means of going any further with this."

One far-fetched theory emanating from Saad's working life is that he was targeted by Iranian spies desperate to get their hands on high-resolution satellite technology. Saad operated in that field, and did computer-assisted design work for Surrey

Satellite Technology Limited (SSTL), based in Guildford. This theory revolved around the notion that Saad was selling industry secrets to Iran, or perhaps to other nations who might want to harm the West.

SSTL is owned by EADS, the European Aeronautic Defence and Space Company. EADS has since been renamed Airbus Defence and Space.

The company started when a group of scientists from the University of Surrey put their own satellite into orbit in 1981, with the help of NASA. The fledgling company galvanised its global reputation when it helped to develop the TopSat programme, the UK's first military surveillance satellite, for the Ministry of Defence. Since the launch of that imaging satellite in 2005, it has been involved in projects for many different countries. They include Nigeria, Thailand, China, Chile, Turkey, Malaysia and Algeria. Its technological advances have enabled smaller countries which cannot afford space programmes to have the opportunity to launch smaller micro-satellites which can be used for surveillance over foreign territory.

On its website SSTL boasts how its 25 years of experience in this niche field make it "the world's premier provider of operational and commercial satellite programmes".

SSTL not only designs and manufactures satellites; it also carries through projects up to launch and operation. The website describes how it can "deliver complete mission solutions for remote sensing, science, navigation and telecommunications". The company now promotes its technology around the world. In total, SSTL has launched 34 spacecraft, with 13 more currently under manufacture.

Anyone capable of divulging sensitive information about satellite design and launch would seem to be an extremely valuable spy for operatives working for a country like Iran. Surveillance satellites are absolutely crucial tools in all modern conflicts.

Saad, though, was never actually on the company's salaried staff. He worked freelance, picking up fixed-term contracts. SSTL was simply his most consistent employer over the 12 months prior to his death. There had been many others too. Family friend and fellow engineer James Mathews said the last major project Saad had worked on was designing the galley kitchen of the new Airbus. This was also confirmed by his Claygate-based accountant Julian Steadman. Mr Mathews also said Saad earned £28,000 in the most recent financial year, not the salary you would expect someone holding high value secrets to command.

Gary Aked, who first met Saad when they worked together in the early 1990s, is firmly of the view that his friend's work could never have put him in danger.

"He wanted to work on engineering projects without the politics that went on in some defence areas," Gary said in 2012. "He has never worked at any other company that I know of that has given him sensitive work to do."

Mr Steadman also had regular chats with his client about his source of income. There was nothing suspicious about it so far as he was concerned.

"He was designing a kitchen galley for an aircraft down in Brighton," Mr Steadman informed me. "People were jumping up and down thinking it was secret aircraft work but it was just commercial work. As far as I knew there was nothing military involved. He was a very accomplished engineer and designer. Anything to do with electronics or mechanics he could do really."

Not long after the murders it was suggested that Saad had been working on a secret aeronautical project at SSTL. The Mail on Sunday claimed that part of his role was with the company's renowned digital imaging enterprise, based close to its headquarters. It was also alleged that the Guildford -based firm had been "of interest" to MI5 for ten years, with the agency conducting surveillance on British-based individuals who made contact with the firm. One unnamed security expert was quoted as saying: "The Iranians are desperate to acquire cutting-edge technology, which they cannot legally obtain. If they were either getting it from Mr al-Hilli, or hoped to get it from him and he refused, they would not think twice about killing him."

But Shreen Ayob, a close friend of Saad's, said she and others who knew the al-Hillis well were infuriated by the suggestion he worked in the defence industry. It simply wasn't true, she said in a blog on the Huffington Post website.

Another former colleague, Derek Reed, was also quick to play down any suggestions that the murders could have been in anyway connected to Saad's job. Just a few days after the attack, Mr Reed said: "We are all shocked and absolutely baffled by what could be behind this. Certainly nothing about his work would have put him at risk. He would not have had to sign the Official Secrets Act for what he was doing. I don't think there were any special precautions put into place to keep him safe because of anything he did at work."

There has never been any independent corroboration of any of the claims about Saad's work.

Former CEO Dr Matt Perkins paid tribute to the highly respected engineer. "Saad worked at SSTL as a Mechanical Design Engineer from November 2010. Saad's colleagues will remember him as an experienced and committed engineer who worked as part of a tightly knit team. He was a personal friend to many of our staff here."

Perhaps of more relevance than SSTL to the inquiry are jobs Saad did many years before his death. In the 1980s he carried out work at the Rutherford Appleton Laboratory nuclear research department in Oxfordshire. The tightly-guarded lab employs 1,200 staff and provides support for more than 10,000 scientists and engineers. It was reported that Saad first went there on a work experience placement while studying for his degree at Kingston University. Regarded as bright and hard-working, he was also said to have gone back in subsequent summers.

Gary Aked, who worked for four years at the Atomic Weapons Establishment, later confirmed this.

Saad later started his own aeronautics design business, Shtech Ltd, the name presumably an acronym for Saad Hilli Tech, in 2001. He ran it from his Claygate home, setting up a workshop in the garden outhouse. Saad's expertise was such that Gary was eager to set up in partnership with him. His knowledge was respected by all those who worked with him. But there was a problem which seemed to have prohibited him from working in projects which might involve sensitive secrets – his Iraqi background.

"I remember he was building this enormous shed which was going to be his office," Gary recalled. "That was after he got married and had the children. He wanted to set up his business from this office. I helped him put in the doors and windows. He had this enormous A0 printer in the office. He said it was to print something out to show clients. He wanted everything there. I seriously considered working with Saad. I was a chartered mechanical design engineer and Saad was always very envious of that. I'd also been working on defence projects. He said that if I came in and worked with him he would be able to get the business with my background. I thought this would be brilliant. I wouldn't have to go out and get the work."

If industrial espionage were a plausible explanation for what happened above Chevaline, then comparisons can be drawn with the murder of another British family in France in August 1952. That notorious case took place at another picturesque village, Lurs, about four hours south of Chevaline. At the time it too created shocking front-page news.

The bodies of Sir Jack Drummond, a prominent government scientist, his wife, Anne, and daughter Elizabeth, 10, were discovered following a horrific massacre. Elizabeth had been bludgeoned to death with a blunt instrument; the parents had been shot with a former US Army rifle. What made the case intriguing for many years afterwards was that a local farmer who initially confessed to the crime later withdrew his drunken statement. His death sentence was commuted and he was freed from jail in 1960.

One of the theories surrounding Sir Jack's murder was that he had been carrying out surveillance at a nearby agrochemicals factory. At the time he was employed by Boots Ltd to direct research into fertilisers and weed-killers. There was also a suggestion he was meeting a member of the wartime French resistance to reclaim a consignment of gold provided by Britain. As has proved the case with Saad al-Hilli, many people did not believe Sir Jack was simply in the area on holiday.

The answer about the relevance of Saad's work perhaps lies with the secret services, from whom the detectives have attempted to extract background information on Saad. Whether this amounts to much remains frustratingly unclear. Shortly after the murders, one of the al-Hillis' Claygate neighbours was quoted as saying Special Branch officers had been monitoring Saad's home. Philip Murphy, a retired finance director, recalled then how police asked if they could use his driveway to spy on the massacre victims' mock-Tudor property about nine years previously. He said: "I watched them from the window and they were watching Mr al-Hilli and his brother. I thought they were from Special Branch. They would sit there all day in their parked car just looking at the house. When Mr al-Hilli came out and drove off, they would follow him. It was all very odd. I never told the family they were being watched."

This was prior to Saad working for SSTL, but might still be linked to both his professional and ethnic background. When I contacted Mr Murphy recently, he refused to elaborate on those initial comments.

Monsieur Maillaud and his team are still struggling to ascertain whether there is any foundation in the suspicion surrounding Saad's employment.

"The others who could help us with this line of inquiry are foreign countries or the secret services, but they are not going to tell us anything," he said. "We have put the question to secret services in France and in the UK. In both cases they gave us a certain amount of information, the minimum, and then it ceased completely. Of course this poses the question of whether they are holding something back, but not necessarily. That is how the secret service works. The secret services were aware of Saad, they knew the name, but perhaps they decided there was nothing interesting about him."

Chapter 19

Seventh theory: Saddam's hidden millions

If, as Zaid al-Hilli insists, the mystery of the Chevaline massacre cannot be solved in Britain, might it be unravelled in the brothers' birth country, Iraq? It is certainly a place where Saad and Iqbal, who was also Iraqi-born, might have had enemies. Could there be someone in Iraq willing and capable of organising a meticulously planned assassination of them, or even of Iqbal's mother, Suhaila? It is equally plausible her family, the al-Saffars, might have enemies. We know so much less about Iqbal and her mother.

Several journalists have been to Baghdad to investigate Saad's ties with his homeland. They include The Sunday Telegraph's Chief Foreign Correspondent Colin Freeman, who spoke to members of the al-Hilli family still in the Iraqi capital in December 2012. Hussain al-Hilli, Saad's cousin, spoke of Saad as worried and slightly paranoid. During one of their Facebook conversations in February, six months before the murders, Saad told his cousin he wanted to leave England.

"He sounded worried about something, saying he was not feeling OK, and that he wanted to come to live in Iraq," Hussain told the journalist. "I thought: why would an Iraqi who has lived most of his life in England suddenly want to come to live here, when nearly every other Iraqi would love to come and live in England? I didn't ask him much about it at the time. I wish I had now."

Hussain, then 59, was never able to establish the exact cause of Saad's disquiet, but he was able to dispel many of the rumours surrounding the al-Hilli family's past in the Middle East. That speculation revolved around a story in the French newspaper Le Monde headlined: "The potential links between the al-Hillis and Saddam Hussein".

In the article, a French police source was quoted as saying the German secret service had informed anti-terror officers of the financial link between the dictator and Saad's father Kadhim. It stated: "The tensions began after Saad al-Hilli's father was struck off the list of beneficiaries of the former Iraqi dictator." A slightly different version, that the fall-out was just a smokescreen and Kadhim was actually managing Saddam's secret accounts, was also mentioned. Shortly before the despot was executed in 2006, it was revealed that he withdrew around £620million from the Iraqi central bank in 2003. He had started to hide this money around the world when American troops entered Baghdad following Operation Shock and Awe. The assets would have been added to millions already deposited in accounts in other countries - mainly through Iraqis who had moved abroad. Saddam was known to have concentrated considerable funds in Switzerland and France, where he had two homes and a £17million yacht.

Had Saad been well aware of the location of the money somewhere in a secretive Swiss bank? Was that why he had been making so many urgent calls to Switzerland? A crucial role in a web of deceit being targeted by nearly every Western intelligence agency could have made him a target. The French police made no secret of the fact that Saad's Iraqi background was one of the main subjects being investigated.

But contradicting these swirling rumours, Hussain insisted that the Swiss bank account would never have been set up to salt away millions of pounds for hated Saddam.

The reality, according to Hussain, was that the wealthy Iraqi family were actually in London when Saddam's Ba'ath party seized power in a 1968 coup. According to other sources, the boys' great-uncle, a man called Hashim al-Hilli, a diplomat for the previous regime, was arrested and tortured by the dictator's henchmen. Another al-Hilli relative was imprisoned by Saddam's half-brother, Barzan al-Tikriti, who seized shares in his businesses. Kadhim realised he too could face arrest so left with his family.

"The Hilli family were not liked by Saddam, who forced Kadhim to flee and also jailed two other relatives," Hussain insisted in the interview. "It is hurtful for us to hear people say that they were laundering money for him."

"Saddam wanted to nationalise everything and didn't like private businessmen doing anything," added Hussain. "The family were not in a good relationship with the regime. The theory that this was all to do with Saddam's money was baseless."

Dr Zaid Alabdi told me Saad would have had as

much disdain for Saddam as millions of other Iraqis who suffered terribly under the despot's tyrannical reign.

"One of the theories that Maillaud has put in his equation is about the al-Hilli family's relationship with Saddam Hussein," he said. "Saad is Shi'ite and Saddam never liked Shi'ites. If he had done anything with him there would have been money, but there is no money. How did Saddam trust him when they don't trust Shi'ites? They were excluded from everything. That is something that I find difficult to believe. The day Saddam died Saad was happy like most of us."

Emmanuel Ludot, a French lawyer who defended Saddam Hussein following his capture, also dismissed the notion of the dictator's hidden fortune as fantasy.

Another disputed allegation centred on a secret trust thought to contain up to £15million in illegal kickbacks to Saddam and his cronies. Unnamed intelligence sources were quoted as saying the trust was set up in the European tax haven of Liechtenstein. It was said to be used to hide money skimmed off from the controversial UN food-for-oil aid programme. This was a scheme established in the 1990s to allow Iraq to sell oil on the world market in exchange for food, medicine, and other humanitarian needs for ordinary Iraqis, without allowing the country to boost its military capabilities. Later it was discovered the corrupt Ba'ath party hierarchy was selling oil to neighbouring Middle East nations and making billions of pounds through illegal surcharges. The money was mostly hidden in accounts abroad in countries with secretive banking laws such as Switzerland and Liechtenstein. In one newspaper article it was claimed that Saad was waiting for further instructions from Baghdad, but the communication never materialised. This claim has never been corroborated.

The French police have certainly taken the Iraqi money connection seriously enough to undertake considerable investigations. They have come up with little reward though, and have been frustrated by red tape and a lack of co-operation in Iraq.

"More than anything, we wanted to go to Iraq to look into the origins of the fortune of Kadhim, the father," Monsieur Maillaud told me. "There are perhaps others in Iraq but we have been limited in our investigations there. We have however been able to speak to members of the family all over the world, and they have given a lot of details of what we might find in Iraq."

The man leading the French team also told me his police squad have found accounts in the name of the father Kadhim in British tax havens Jersey and Guernsey. "The origin of the money is undoubtedly unclear," he said.

"Another strange thing is that the Iraqi ambassador in France himself offered to help us out," the prosecutor continued. "He promised an enormous amount of information, notably on arms trafficking and other useful areas. We are looking at very remote theories like an Italian who was paid to execute Iraqis in a foreign country. Here was a theory that sounded intellectually coherent. I spoke to him on the phone twice, and so did several other judges involved in the investigation. The principle of co-operation was active but at the moment we actually wanted to do something there was silence. We couldn't get him on the phone. Of course this made us ask questions. Why would one offer help and then suddenly refuse? It's bizarre. And of course we can't arrest the ambassador if we think he might be hiding something."

Despite all of these mysterious hold-ups, the French team have reached the conclusion the lack of co-operation is down to inefficiency, not a conspiracy to thwart their attempts at finding the motive for the Chevaline murders.

"The idea that the brothers' father had stolen the money from Saddam Hussein and put it in Switzerland does not seem credible to me," Monsieur Maillaud affirmed. "The accounts of Saddam Hussein were in hundreds of millions of dollars, whereas this account had only €1million. It's a derisory sum for Saddam Hussein. There is no sense in that theory, but the idea that it could be the profit from the sale of his businesses in Iraq is a lot more believable. Here there are plenty of questions too. Why would the Iraqi state, to avenge Kadhim al-Hilli, have killed his son, and, therefore, why would they not kill Zaid? There are so many questions that it does not seem the theory to put at the top of the list."

After fleeing to England and later the Costa del Sol for a life in exile, Kadhim only rarely returned to his homeland. But, according to elder brother Zaid, Saad went back twice, once with their mother and once alone. Others have told me the visits were more regular. The first time Saad had gone back to Iraq was in 2003, nine years before his death. He didn't travel for leisure but with a determined purpose: to check on the condition of the old family home armed with the original deeds in Arabic script. If he was hoping for a swift resolution he did not get one. The gated villa was in Baghdad's elite Adhamiyah district, a wealthy neighbourhood favoured by the Iraqi elite during Saddam's iron-fist rule. After the despot was removed from power in the second Iraq war, Adhamiyah became a hotbed of the insurgency. The walls of the luxurious mansions which lined the banks of the River Tigris were pockmarked with bullet holes, and it was considered one of the most likely places to be shot at or abducted in the conflict-torn country. The streets were ripped up by IED bombs and thousands of ordinary people moved out. Shopkeepers kept their stores shuttered up.

When Saad got to the villa it was only a very short time after Saddam's downfall, in fact it was in the same weeks of December 2003 that the deposed leader was located down a hole near the city of Tikrit by US forces.

Hussain recalled his hot-headed cousin went to the house alone and immediately got involved in an argument with members of another family who had taken it over.

"A woman answered the door and started shouting at him," Hussain remembered Saad telling him. "Two men started kicking him and punching him. Saad came home bleeding from the head. When I saw him I told him: 'Are you crazy? You should never have gone there alone, you could have got killed. But Saad was a quite a confrontational guy, and he liked to fight for his rights. Later he told me that he had got the house back. When I asked him how, he just said: 'I used some connections.'"

Dr Alabdi was also told by Saad he had done something to resolve the problem, but not what. "I remember asking him about the house in Iraq about a year after he came back," he recalled. "He just said, 'Let's say it's been sorted'. That was all; it was very unlike him. It's all mystery."

Another of Saad's cousins, a woman named Balsam, said in 2012 the family in the villa were actually there with the owner's permission. They were a respectable lawyer and his wife, who finally decided to leave in 2004 when the insurgency was at its nadir.

Today the property is believed to be empty.

It is difficult to determine whether Saad's practically suicidal mission to Baghdad to reclaim what he believed was rightfully his might have led to his own death. He certainly seemed to think there was some danger: it was for that reason he bought the Taser which Surrey Police discovered in Claygate after his death.

Such a theory, among the many that exist, seems very far-fetched. The al-Hilli family villa, badly damaged by years of neglect, would not be worth such an extravagant sum that anyone could consider it worth setting up a contract killing in Europe.

Could Saad really have done something drastic enough in Baghdad for someone to hunt him down to the French Alps?

Chapter 20

Eighth theory: Suhaila's dangerous son and a Swedish mystery

The focus of most of the theories, most of the news stories and even most of the police investigation concerning the Chevaline killings has centred squarely on Saad al-Hilli. After him, the cyclist Sylvain Mollier has been considered the next most likely target, and then Saad's wife Iqbal. Suhaila al-Allaf, Saad's mother-in-law, has been subject to by far the least scrutiny. Perhaps because of her age, perhaps because she was a very private person who lived in Sweden and was rarely photographed, Suhaila's life has remained obscure.

She was born in Iraq in 1938. As a young woman she studied at Royal Holloway College, in Egham, Surrey, and obtained a PhD in biology. Nor was that her first time in the country: it is believed that as a child her well-educated family were in

England for a time. It should be remembered that Iraq had longstanding colonial ties with Iraq, so the path of professionals from Baghdad to London was well-trodden.

Suhaila married an Iraqi named Abdul al-Saffar and had four children: Iqbal in 1965, Haydar, a boy, in 1966, their sister Fadwa and brother Ahmed Mahmood.

After Iqbal completed her dentistry course at Baghdad University some time around 1986 the family dispersed. Suhaila, Abdul and their son Haydar settled in Tumba, in the southern suburbs of Swedish capital Stockholm. Iqbal was in the UAE by the late 1990s and Fadwa was studying pharmacology at Reading University. Ahmed's career is less well known, but in my conversations with Saad's friends, they have intimated he was less than complimentary towards that brother-in-law. It was Haydar to whom the police's attention was first drawn. In fact, the hypothesis that he might have been the perpetrator was widely circulated in the immediate aftermath.

Haydar was also in Britain in the weeks before the massacre, apparently in the care of a psychiatric hospital. He had long-term mental health problems which had led to alleged violent psychotic episodes and brought him to the attention of the authorities in Sweden several times. I have obtained Swedish police reports that give an insight into why the French police were very interested in Haydar as they tried to piece together potential causes of the merciless bloodbath.

Haydar had a history of allegedly attacking his own family. He had also been missing for several weeks before he was seemingly tracked down to the psychiatric hospital in England.

A Swedish police report from Sunday June 24, 2007, concerns a call-out over an alleged domestic dispute between Haydar and his father Abdul at the flat in Tumba. In the report it was stated that Abdul told police his son, who had lived with them his whole life, had obsessive-compulsive disorder and schizophrenia. They wrote that the son was "very controlling and won't let the parents do what they want", adding he had "over a long period subjected his parents to threats, hitting and other violations".

In the same report it was claimed that Haydar threatened to become even more violent if officers took him into custody at the nearest police station. It was said that the flat was "in a mess", so the officers took the decision not to quiz Suhaila. The report detailed three other instances of alleged violence against Suhaila and Abdul by Haydar, one in 2004 and two in 2006. The most recent had again been for assault. The report stated that Haydar was an extremely strong and heavy man, weighing 19 stone. This made him nearly twice his 10 stone father's weight.

Dad Abdul, who died in 2011, was on dialysis at the time for his liver, and also suffered kidney problems.

The detailed report said: "He is constantly threatening his parents and he is very argumentative. He uses abusive language and physically abuses them. Today he hit Abdul on the head and with an open hand; afterwards Abdul felt dizzy and faint. After he had hit him he also pushed him. He also hit his mother on the head twice."

Haydar told police the alleged fracas was sparked by a row over his complaining the television was too loud during breakfast. After Haydar struck out, Suhaila entered the room and retaliated with her walking stick, the report stated. Haydar alleged his parents were abusing him but officers discounted his version.

In a 2005 report. Haydar was reported to have squeezed his father's wrists, where Abdul had previously had surgery. The report claimed that when his father tried to leave his flat, Haydar grabbed his walking stick and pointed it at him saying "I can kill you". Crucially, the official report alleged, Abdul did not trust his own son.

"Haydar has pushed, hit, threatened them and made them do things against their will," the officers wrote. "During the last year this has happened on a daily basis. For example Haydar will order his parents to sit completely still and if they fail to do so he will hit them. He has also ordered them to stop washing up, not watch TV and so on. During these instances Haydar has called his parents obscene things."

There was also a report of an assault by Haydar in May 2007 when he allegedly hit his father in the chest and head, as well as kicking him in the stomach. As a dialysis patient, such blows could have proved fatal to Abdul. It was also claimed Haydar twisted his father's arms very hard and before the assault started he allegedly threatened his father and said "no one can do anything to me and I want to kill you".

On another occasion Haydar allegedly pushed his parents around while they were in their local town centre. "Both the father and mother are really scared of their son and they want to report a crime of assault and threat," they wrote. Another time, Suhaila "locked herself into a room in order to get away from her violent and aggressive son".

"Haydar is mentally ill and he blames his

parents for this," the report authors suggest. "He claims that they did not look after and nurture him during his childhood." But they also said he was refusing to take his prescribed medication.

Suhaila and Abdul allegedly told police they believed Haydar was schizophrenic, that he had terrorised them since 2001 and that threats were made on a daily basis.

The court papers showed Haydar was never charged over the alleged assaults because both Suhaila and Abdul refused to testify against him.

Questions remain about Haydar. Suhaila had been staying with her other daughter Fadwa until the night before the al-Hilli family left for France, when Saad picked her up from Reading. But why was Haydar in the country? And if he was held in a psychiatric unit, why?

But less than the ten days after the killings, an inquiry source was quoted as saying the theory Haydar might be the culprit had been "put away in a drawer". Haydar was in England when the murders happened. It was concluded he would not have been capable of orchestrating the execution of his mother, sister and brother-in-law.

Nevertheless, here was another intriguing element to the complex family histories of the three murder victims in the estate car. None of the victims, it appeared, had straight-forward backgrounds.

A measure of doubt still lingers around Suhaila and her presence on the holiday – and therefore at the scene of the massacre. Was it simply an act of kindness on Saad's part for her to be away with her grand-daughters? I have been told that Suhaila was intending to set up a bank account, perhaps in Switzerland, for Zainab and Zeena. It has been suggested this would have been a large sum of money, something to help them when they got older. She only had one other grandchild, through her son Ahmed, but played little part in that child's upbringing. Suhaila was devoted to the girls and was delighted to be with them in France.

Could a decision to give away a large chunk of her savings to the girls have antagonised other family members?

Or did a happy family visit prompt jealous feelings that twisted into murderous ones? Saad and Iqbal had taken their daughters to meet Suhaila in Sweden in 2011. It was a happy time for both sides of the family.

Suhaila's nephew Hasan Ahmad al-Saffar, 18 at the time of the killings, said in the immediate aftermath: "We had a lovely time together when they visited us a year ago. We took them around Stockholm to see the sights with the children, who were just two wonderful little girls. Saad was a really loving father. He really took care of his daughters. Iqbal was a doting mother and the children were so well behaved. We have no idea why this has happened or what led to it."

Might Haydar perhaps have witnessed this affection from Suhaila towards her grand-daughters? Could that have prompted him to kill his own mother following the death of his father Abdul the previous year? It certainly seems highly implausible. But there remain some strange happenings surrounding Suhaila.

One troubling detail is that so-called spyware was found on her personal computer, a program that enabled whoever installed it to remotely view everything she did on the terminal. Some third party had the capability to see every email she wrote and every website she visited.

Equally worrying, Suhaila's flat in Tumba, southern Stockholm, has been burgled. A French police source told me a large cache of significant items have been taken, including documents that might have assisted their inquiries. Papers related to her bank accounts and the al-Hilli family allegedly went missing. A computer also apparently disappeared. Ahmad al-Saffar, Suhaila's brother-in-law, has been questioned about the burglary, prosecutor Eric Maillaud told me.

Mr al-Saffar, an academic in the Department of Medical Sciences at Uppsala University, is an interesting figure because according to French police sources he accompanied Fadwa when she went to Grenoble to see Zainab while she was in a coma and provide solace for bewildered Zeena. He was also at the al-Hillis funeral and played an influential role in trying to secure appropriate care for Zainab and Zeena after they were brought back to Britain.

I have repeatedly tried to contact Mr al-Saffar at home and at the university, but he has not responded. Haydar has not been quizzed in relation to this project.

"We have no explanation for this spyware in the mother-in-law's computer," Monsieur Maillaud told me. "We found some software on her computer that allows someone to remotely follow everything that happens on that computer. Why, we are not sure. This is something anyone could install, but you would need to be quite good at IT. Saad al-Hilli could have done it with his eyes closed, but not the mother-in-law. This of course conjures up a lot of suspicion. Why would someone want to keep tabs on someone else's computer? It is part of the mystery. We also have the fact that her home in the Stockholm suburbs was robbed and ransacked. We know some stuff was taken but we don't know what else might have been stolen.

"It's true that there is a slight mystery surrounding the mother-in-law, but we have even less understanding of how she could be the target," Monsieur Maillaud continued. "It's extremely remote. She was not a rich woman. Of course, when she left Iraq she would have left with all her money in cash, so it is hard to trace, but there is nothing remarkable about that if you flee a country. Maybe there was some money hidden in her apartment.

"Of course we have asked whether the target could have been the grandmother. It's true that she could have been. There are strange things, notably that her home was ransacked and robbed. A computer disappeared. Little things like that about which I haven't spoken before are also lines of questioning. When you go to a crime scene, you have to consider that all of them, even the children, could have been the target. That is why we have dug so much into everyone's lives."

Chapter 21

Conclusion: who was the Chevaline killer?

When I first went to Chevaline on the day of the murders, I knew next to nothing about the victims of the Annecy massacre. Today, I have spent several months uncovering as much as I can about them. But as I try to make sense of the various conflicting theories surrounding the deaths of those four people at that remote clearing on September 5, 2012, each theory competes for attention, and each victim. A theory that might have seemed far and away the most plausible explanation is knocked from its pedestal at the top of the crime-board by a new snippet of information. But nonetheless my research has brought me to a position where I feel confident in putting forward what seems to me the most realistic explanation for these most unlikely killings in that most unlikely location.

To do this, I must first discount all those theories that now seem to me improbable.

The police in France have three main hypotheses: one, that cyclist Sylvain Mollier was the target; two, that the al-Hillis were the targets; three that none was the target and they were all in the wrong place at the wrong time. Hundreds of police officers have been involved in the pan-European investigation for endless months and are still no nearer one definitive scenario that fits all the evidence, so it would be foolhardy of me, working alone, to claim I have come up with better.

In my opinion, however, the possibility that Sylvain Mollier was the intended target, and the al-Hillis the innocent bystanders, seems less conceivable than the other way around. Sylvain was of course the local man. He was someone who would have been easier for a local enemy – a love rival or a member of his extended family with a grudge – to trace from his home in Ugine up to Le Martinet. But such a senseless loss of life for personal matters that had created no big waves in the local community previously is just too much of a leap of imagination. He was on OK terms with his ex-wife and reportedly received a phone call from her on his mobile during his last cycle ride. He saw his two sons from that relationship all the time. He was not going to inherit his new partner's wealth, and she was not as fabulously rich as first claimed. Possibly, as prosecutor Eric Maillaud implied to me, Sylvain was a ladies' man who might have annoyed a few guys of similar age in close-knit Ugine. But such enmity would more likely be settled by a fist fight outside the Carrefour supermarket in the small town of 7,000 people, not an execution.

And, quite frankly, a clearly highly professional killer bungling so badly that he had to kill three inconvenient witnesses (four if the intention was to kill Zainab) is hard to credit. This was a killer who left no trace evidence at the scene, and no trace of himself in the woods and roads around.

Zaid, Saad's brother, is driven by the view that Mollier was the intended target, but the theory seems to be based more on a distrust of the French investigators than on any sound reasoning or evidence. He told me there was a "conspiracy to cover it up" from the first time police searched his flat on September 28, 2012, long before his eventual arrest.

Asked why Mollier would be the target, and not his

brother, he could only say: "Well, he's out of their hair, isn't he? He's not going to cause them any problems, now or in the future. You must look at the future and the problems he would have caused for the people around him. It's all been kept hushed up, rightly, but we should have been treated in the same way."

To me, this sense of unfairness was the main reason he thought the authorities must be protecting Mollier. Zaid has a point - he has been very publicly thrown to the lions in a way that none of Sylvain Mollier's relatives have - but I think it is stretching the imagination to suggest Monsieur Maillaud's unequal treatment of the two affected families amounts to a deliberate cover-up. I simply cannot believe it.

This brings me on to the theory of a local madman, a psychotic patient on release or a far-right extremist being the killer. These do not add up either. Instances in which someone imbalanced carries out a mass murder then somehow slips quietly back into their local community are very rare. That would require steely composure. I cannot believe all of those victims were merely in the wrong place at the wrong time.

And why would a racist, chancing upon and

then slaughtering the al-Hillis several kilometres beyond Chevaline, then make no statement about the murders? The attack on a visiting family of Arab extraction would be rendered a completely meaningless gesture for someone in pursuit of such a misguided, hateful cause. This is something Zaid also pointed out to me. "The French police told me they were also looking at psychopaths and racists," he commented. "They started coming up with this because it's always handy to make it look so vague. I did say to them, 'These psychopaths, if you look at what happens in America, or that mass murder in Norway, they want to be known. They don't hide in bushes and shoot a number of people. A psychopath might attack a woman, like the jogger on Wimbledon Common a few years back, but it's usually one person, not a number of people. I didn't buy their story. It's absolute rubbish. And why would a racist be hiding in a forest for a foreign car? They could be hiding for a week there!"

Zaid's opinion is a well-constructed argument with which it is hard to disagree.

Similarly, the theory of the al-Hillis disturbing an illicit exchange like a drug deal seems ludicrous.

During my return visit to Chevaline for this book I spent an hour with Didier Bertholllet, mayor at the time of the murders. “We said it could be a madman, or a mistake, or a local criminal,” he said. “Someone here said it was somewhere people go to do drug deals, but that is rubbish. There are not a lot of clients up there!”

The next theory in logical sequence is that of a local gun collector, someone similar in profile to Eric Devouassoux, being the killer. As Monsieur Maillaud pointed out, the choice of mass-produced and widely distributed Swiss Army Luger P06 gun would make it extremely difficult indeed to find such a killer. The problem with this theory, as with the racist killing line of inquiry, is that it supposes the murderer carried out the most heinous slaughter in the Annecy region in history and then simply melted back into normality. To me that seems just as unbelievable. Someone would have heard something – a wife, a mate, a colleague. There would have been a slip of the tongue following a few drinks at a barbecue or at a summer boules tournament.

This is no amateur job. Word always gets out; unless the killer has been trained, as the special forces in the military are, not to brag. Anyone who knows about the military tends to say the elite of the SAS are the ones who never talk about killing. The ones who sit at the bar telling Rambo-style war stories are the Walter Mitty characters, the frauds.

A killer with a military background?

As we shall see again, the killer's likely escape up the mountain track across rough terrain more likely means the killer must have had, or quickly attained, deep local knowledge. A local killer?

In fact, I have been provided with new information that reinforces the notion of this killer being local, and possibly someone with a military background.

The first potential insight into the way detectives are currently thinking came to me through the French investigative team. It concerned the suicide of a former member of the Foreign Legion, from Ugine, Sylvain's home town. The 50-year-old's death at his own hand in June 2014 has been previously reported, but its significance has never been properly explored.

I have been told the man's first name Francois, but police will not confirm this. He had been working as a fireman in the Alpine town after more than 20 years in the ultra-tough Legion. He had been a parachutist, serving in the field of battle in some of the world's nastiest trouble-spots. He would have engaged the enemy in conflicts in the Ivory Coast, Somalia, Bosnia and Rwanda. He would no doubt have witnessed some horrific sights.

In April 2013 the man, who lived alone in a block of flats, was interviewed about the murders in a very routine and friendly 45-minute questioning as police followed up every possible lead. He was known to the Schutz family, Monsieur Maillaud told me, but he was never someone they thought at the time could be the killer. Yet in his suicide letter, found at the flat, he complained he felt he was being accused of the Chevaline murders.

"The hypothesis near the top of the chain for the investigators is a local killing," Monsieur Maillaud told me. "We have a real suspect. I am referring to the Legionnaire from Ugine who committed suicide. For me, this remains a real mystery because you have a military man who for years was in the Foreign Legion, which often attracts tough people, who might have previously committed crimes. Here is a middle-aged man who kills himself and to explain his act leaves a letter. In the letter he says he could not handle being considered a suspect capable of carrying out these killings. This is strange. We are talking about a hardened ex-soldier, someone used to using a gun, suddenly saying he couldn't deal with being thought of as a suspect. For me, this is very interesting. In his two-page letter he explains in more detail that he felt like he was being charged over this murder because he was interviewed by a gendarme. When we went back to read through his interview, we realised it wasn't one carried out under caution. He was not being considered a suspect, just a witness. I struggle to believe that a tough guy, someone who drank a lot, someone who got in fights in bars, someone who probably spent a few days behind bars in the military jail, cannot then put up with 45 minutes of polite interview with a police officer."

The prosecutor confirmed detectives are still digging into the man's past because of what seems from the outside like an abrupt, illogical suicide. Monsieur Maillaud has asked officers to "pursue this line of inquiry as far as possible". He said that the man suffered "psychological problems" caused by his long service for the Foreign Legion.

"Could it, by chance, have been him?" he asked. "Did he regret his actions afterwards and take his own life? He did not admit responsibility in his suicide letter, but for me it is a suicide that seems to be connected to what happened. This was the suicide of someone who had the technical capacity to do what was done that day."

Here is one individual who fits the precise profile of the Chevaline killer. If it were not the Ugine Legionnaire, then I believe it has to be another assassin with a similar background, someone skilled enough and callous enough to use a pistol with such efficacy. As has previously been described, the act of changing the gun's magazine twice virtually rules out anyone not an expert.

There is also fresh data collated by police on both sides of the Channel that reinforces the idea the killer was someone who knew the area. If not a French or Swiss assassin, then a "low-cost" hired hand who had done his homework sufficiently to make his escape over the other side of the mountain from Le Martinet.

French police have scanned thousands of hours of CCTV footage of Saad's distinctive maroon BMW estate from the moment it left the Claygate house a few days before the murders. British police obtained footage of the car on the motorway, at a petrol station and at the Dover ferry terminal as the al-Hillis made their crossing to France. French police did the same, recovering many tapes of the car getting off the ferry, stopping at service stations, passing through town centres and at the toll booths which are at regular intervals throughout the French motorway network. At none of them has the same vehicle been seen in close proximity to the al-Hillis' car.

This does not rule out a "professional" assassination, but it does almost certainly rule out the idea of the al-Hillis being stalked all the way from Claygate to Chevaline. The killer, however, must have known where they were staying in order to follow them up the Combe d'Ire road from the campsite. Someone who knew Saad, Iqbal or Suhaila's movements well enough needed to have given the assassin sufficient warning to be in place at the time. Saad had tracker software on his computer, enabling those to whom he gave access to follow his movements. There might have been several people aware of where he was. Police will not divulge further details.

And what of Iqbal? She told friends she did not use email, that she was technologically incompetent, and yet Jimmy Thompson's relatives in the United States claim she retained a secret email relationship with him over a decade.

Here we return to the initial eye-witness reports of a mysterious man seen lurking around the campsite. Some said Saad was seen in a heated discussion with the man, thought to be of "Balkans" appearance. A source close to the inquiry said to me the notion of a "low-cost killer" from former Yugoslavia is an option still under consideration. To me this suggestion seems believable.

"This is coherent with the notion of them being followed by a vehicle driven by someone who took advantage of the isolation of the spot to carry out an execution," Monsieur Maillaud told me. "It supposes a meticulous level of organisation. To imagine a professional killer who intended to kill the al-Hilli family waiting in his 4x4 car is difficult. It would have been easier if he had been working with the motorcyclist. Nothing is impossible. Perhaps he waited, killed them and then carried on the other way where no one saw him except the forestry worker."

Ex-Chevaline mayor Monsieur Berthollet, a former P&O Ferries captain, said someone who knew of the restricted route from the lay-by could have been on the other side of the mountain in an hour. "It would be easy to escape that way," he confirmed.

It is important to remember at this point that the police's view is that the murderer was still at or very near the scene when British cyclist Brett Martin arrived there. In other words, the killer would have passed Brett and the French hikers who he found further down the road to make his getaway. If he did not pass the no-entry sign and over the other side of the mountain marked "no access to cars", he would have been seen.

"The day it happened, the police blocked all the routes towards the lake," Monsieur Berthollet explained to me. "But on the other side the killer could have disappeared. You can continue in a 4x4 and then go down the other side quite easily. Or you could walk; even use a mountain bike. It's an easy place to escape. One hour afterwards he would be over the other side."

My instinct was always that Saad had taken the family up the Combe d'Ire track, over the gushing stream through the forest, for a pre-arranged clandestine meeting. It seemed such a strange, out-of-the-way place to be. Yet this is challenged by the evidence from the Solitaire du Lac campsite. Zainab, it seems, wanted to go for a walk in the forest. Were she and her dad looking at a walking route sign at the layby when the killer fired? That seems perfectly logical. But even if their presence up the little-used road was an accident it does not preclude Saad having business somewhere in the region, perhaps in Geneva where his father Kadhim's bank account still lay untouched. Interested parties might well have known the family were staying in Lake Annecy. From there, it would be a case of waiting for the right moment to strike.

There is, also, a further possibility, one that has not really been alluded to in all of the coverage of this case. It is one that would be exceedingly difficult to prove, and one that would be extremely tough for those affected to accept.

Suppose Saad al-Hilli hired the hitman himself? Suppose the assassination of Saad, his wife and his mother-in-law was all the computer engineer's own idea? The killings would effectively be a multiple murder-suicide, by professional hitman.

This notion was put to me by someone who has spent a lot of time studying the case. At first I considered it absolutely unthinkable, preposterous even. But then I was reminded of the appalling regularity of tragic cases in which fathers have decided to take not just their own lives but the lives of their loved ones. Once a year at least there is a news story of this nature at which readers shake their heads in horror and pity. They are infinitely more common, certainly, that Mossad hits on British citizens.

There are obvious objections. First, what in this scenario would explain the fact that one child, Zeena, was forgotten or ignored? Second, if Saad were so distressed for whatever reason – the pressures wrought by fatherhood, money, work, the feud with his brother, the house, his wife's ongoing communication with her first husband – why did he not take his own life and Iqbal's at home?

This outlandish theory would, however, explain what took the al-Hillis to the lay-by and why there seems no evidence of their being followed there by their killer. But such a complex plan does seem unlikely in the extreme. Another symptom perhaps of when nothing is proven, the most unlikely things seem plausible.

So, sticking my neck out, I think the most likely killer was a hitman, hired to kill one or several members of the al-Hilli family, with good knowledge of Chevaline and the mountain range beyond. A local man with a military background… and a purpose.

The Foreign Legion attracts tough guys, loners, criminals with hidden pasts, men without ties, men on the run or leaving their wives and families behind, men desperate enough to sign up for a minimum five-year tour of duty which could involve being barracked in the hostile desert of Djibouti in West Africa. To get into the Foreign Legion you have to be prepared to kill not out of patriotism, not to protect your own nation (most members are not French), but simply because your commanding officer tells you to do so. An experienced ex-member of the Legion would be an ideal candidate for someone wanting to recruit hitmen. To me it seems very worthwhile for Monsieur Maillaud's team to probe further into the life of the mysterious man from Ugine.

I believe there are several motives relating to the al-Hillis that can be ruled out.

As regards Iqbal, police seem to have reached the right decision in being certain Jimmy Thompson's death on the same day as his ex-wife was mere coincidence. Judy, his sister, is convinced foul-play connects the two, but is unable to say precisely why. I cannot find a reason that makes sense.

Any Mossad connection also sounds highly implausible. And as for there being a longstanding contract on his head because of his father being some kind of conduit for Saddam's millions, there is not a shred of credible evidence for this. Nor is there any evidence linking Saad's visits to Baghdad and the loss of the family home there with his murder years later.

Saad's employment at the satellite firm SSTL, and his potential access to secrets that might interest a country like Iran are intriguing aspects to this case. But these background details on his CV are probably no more than that. If Iran or any other country once judged as a rogue state wanted to acquire satellite technology to spy on its enemies, then there must be far easier ways to get hold of it than hijacking a man during a family caravanning holiday to France. From everything you hear about Saad, he simply did not have the time to orchestrate such a plot in any case. He was up to his ears in childcare, building outhouses, customising his children's bikes and helping out his neighbours. He was messaging mates on Skype half the night when he was not buying second-hand goods on eBay. In fact, the more I learned about Saad al-Hilli, the more I wished I had met him. From all the anecdotes, he sounds a very likeable character.

There is no chance Iqbal's nephew Haydar, who was not in the country, was the person responsible for the murders despite his violent tendencies. It is, though, currently impossible to gauge whether the stolen documents and computer at Suhaila's flat have any relevance.

That leaves the feud over money and property between the brothers and Iqbal's secretive past, her bizarre decision to leave the US so suddenly, as the main points of interest.

French police continue to consider Zaid a key

character in this case. As recently as last month two instructing judges – members of the judiciary who guide the French police's inquiries – went to the UK to interview him, I have been told. As has been seen, he still refuses to travel to France to talk to police.

Despite this, however, as one French police source put it to me, if Zaid had really wanted the family fortune then he messed it up. It would have been far simpler for him to have got rid of his brother in Britain, or even Iraq, which they were said to have visited together. But he didn't. Whatever happened regarding their father's will in Geneva, it prompted Saad to take out a caveat blocking his brother from accessing any of the money.

"I have a personal conviction, not necessarily one that is shared by all the investigators, that if he had wanted to harm his brother, then it was his brother alone that he would have wanted to kill, and not the children," Monsieur Maillaud claimed. "The main reason for the hatred of Zaid is a cultural one; it is linked to their Muslim background, to the fact that Zaid is the elder brother. For years, as he was getting old, Kadhim had entrusted Zaid with the management of his fortune and his inheritance, which is of course logical, and in keeping with Islamic tradition. When Saad discovered that Zaid was trying to get money out of their father while he was still alive Kadhim was told by Saad at this point that Zaid wanted to keep the money for himself. It was then that Kadhim was convinced to write out a new will, sharing everything equally. Of that, we are sure. That is why I am personally convinced Zaid must have felt insulted as the elder brother; it was his honour that was at stake. For me, the hate comes from that. I could be wrong though."

Julian Steadman, Saad's accountant, also said to me that there was a dispute between the brothers about their father's will. This was allegedly what prompted Saad to take out the caveat blocking the will from being brought to fruition.

Now, according to Mr Steadman, Zaid has put all of this aside and has agreed that the Oaken Lane house in Claygate is put on the market.

"I've been contacted by Iqbal's sister's solicitors," he told me. "She and Zaid have got together and they are taking action to put the house on the market and clean it up. They are taking out letters of administration for the estate so they can sort it out for the children. That is why I went to the police station, where I saw bags and bags and bags of evidence. I was there for two or three hours shuffling through this stuff. There is an agreement between Zaid and the girls' aunt to get the house on the market because at the moment it's just sitting there rotting. I understand one of the ceilings has come down and I've seen dripping water coming out which I've had to report to the police. I would imagine there's quite a lot to be done before it can be put on the market. I've been able to do the accounts for the company so it can now be put to bed. Whatever is left should go to the children. Saad left no will."

I asked Zaid about this too. He confirmed that the restoration of the Oaken Lane property is underway in the hope it can be put on the market next year. "Hopefully we'll put it on the market soon and the girls will have their inheritance next year," he said. "It's going well."

So the house, the kernel of longstanding friction between two brothers who once loved each other dearly, will soon be up for sale. Zaid, one imagines, will not be pursuing his share given what has happened to the girls. But to me the fact that the fraternal conflict is known about means that inheritance money and property being a motive remains a possibility. In my opinion, despite the fact there is no evidence against Zaid, detectives simply cannot rule out the possibility of the feud being a factor in the executions. Zaid is an innocent man, he was not charged in Britain, but, as we know, he still refuses to travel to Chambéry, where the Chevaline killings operations room is based.

As Monsieur Maillaud told me: "Saad was scared, and he was scared of his brother; we have not invented this. The fact of Saad being scared of his brother is not pure imagination. It is a certitude. Several of his friends have told us how he was scared and had taken quite extreme precautions. This makes us think of Zaid. We are not thinking about him just to persecute the brother. Sincerely, I think it would be dishonest to present it like that. From that point, we cannot move forward."

The second potential motive for me centres on Iqbal. From all I have been told she was a quiet, gentle, inoffensive woman who did her most to integrate into the community in Claygate and, previously, New Orleans. But she and Zaid are the only characters connected to Saad in this saga about whom there have been questions to answer.

I cannot help but wonder why Iqbal went to all the trouble of getting a Green Card in the US and then returning to the United Arab Emirates. Was there another reason for her being in America? Was she involved in anything that could have put her on a hit list, either there in the UAE?

Iqbal is a mystery. Did someone have a reason to target her perhaps? Police interest in that question is probably why, as Dr Zaid Alabdi said to me, British detectives were more interested in the wife than the husband the last time they went to speak with him about his friends, the al-Hillis.

There is still some mystery in the feud between Zaid and Saad and mystery in Iqbal. There is also an element of mystery with regard to Saad's very stressed condition before the French holiday. Zaid was frank with me, but kept returning to the conspiracy theory during our conversation instead of dwelling for too long on the nitty-gritty of the feud with Saad.

There is less mystery in the life of Sylvain Mollier, which detectives have been able to research far more thoroughly. So three conceivable motives, all involving the al-Hilli family; one potential hitman, a well-trained gunman knew the Annecy area well. These are my educated guesses; not certainties.

Eric Maillaud, who has spent more time ruminating on this case than nearly anyone else, candidly concedes his team are still stumped. "This is the problem," he admitted. "With the al-Hilli family, we have stumbled upon a family which is outside of the ordinary. They are an Iraqi refugee family; they had a businessman father who did well during the time of Saddam Hussein. That is of course a source of suspicion outside of Iraq and it provokes a lot of fantasy too. These are the kind of elements that make this like a plot out of a cinema film. If it were a novel, you could write it with many different endings. You could ask the reader to choose their ending."

Chapter 22

An unprecedented investigation

In Chambéry a whole storage vault has been filled with files relating to the al-Hillis and Sylvain Mollier, and there is a similar amount in Guildford. Yet seemingly detectives are still no closer to identifying the culprit.

Might it have been different if the highly criticised French police had acted differently at the outset? Should they have taken the time to focus more on the fundamentals of crime investigation and their analysis of the scene rather than apparently devoting a lot of their manpower to speculative theories about who had ordered the killings and why? There were a few glitches, most notoriously the decision not to search for Zeena in the car at the scene. But it seems unfair to criticise the gendarmerie for this. How could they know there was another child?

Chevaline mayor Didier Berthollet also tells of a few "Keystone Cops" moments on the day the bodies were discovered. Several cars had to turn back because they weren't suitable for the mountain road and one had a flat tyre, he claimed.

Saad's friend James Mathews certainly does not disguise his opinions when it comes to the French-led murder investigation. He cites the alleged failure for a long time to find Saad's passport as one example of the shoddy detective work. When he refers to prosecutor Eric Maillaud, he calls him "the clown". Saad's brother Zaid too has been extremely critical of this and other mistakes. But, many would say, he would be. He was after all arrested very publicly; his reputation has been tarnished.

"If you compare it to Britain, there was recently a case of a guy murdered in Woolwich," Mr Mathews said in our discussion. "The South Circular was closed off for three days even though they had the guy in custody. The forensics took three days. In this case, French forensics spent a matter of hours at the scene. I think they wanted it over quickly because it's not good for tourism having British tourists shot."

Mr Mathews also says he has recent experience of the officers' poor handling and insensitivity towards potential witnesses.

"My wife got a call from them on January 5 this year, 2015," he claimed. "She lives in Germany. She got very upset because they finally decided to interview her. If you had wanted to exclude her from the DNA samples found in the caravan and the house you would think you would do it sooner than two-and-a-half years later. She was Iqbal's best friend. She was very unhappy about it. She hadn't seen them for several years and she couldn't understand why they wanted to talk to her."

Another notable quirk of the investigation was that the police brought down the security cordon less than 48 hours after the crime had been committed. They allowed scores of reporters, photographers and TV crews to trample all over the parking area. This would be unthinkable in Britain.

I was part of the press convoy allowed up to the Le Martinet lay-by that day. It was a truly surreal sight. Several French cameramen were hanging out of the windows of their vans to film the road leading up to what had become the most infamous National Park beauty spot in all of France. I was crammed in the back of a car with several other

Fleet Street reporters. The local gendarmes had restricted the number of vehicles permitted to be at the site. Yet when we got there drivers were allowed to park pretty much wherever they wanted. Any tyre marks on the loose gravel from a getaway vehicle would have been completely ruined.

Once out of the car, I was able to stand at the place where Saad's car had been wedged against the earth bank. Specks of blood were visible on the gravel. There were tiny metal circles embedded in the tarmac with numbers next to them in red permanent marker. It was difficult to know if these were the stray bullets, ricocheted off a tree and stuck in the ground. Photographers and TV crews had sufficient time to get all the footage and images they needed before the police herded us up again and back down the hill.

What was truly peculiar was that the following day the crime scene was sealed off again, and forensic officers were seen heading up the hill. Had they missed something? If so it would surely have been tampered with after the size-10 trainers of the British media had strolled over every inch of this very recent crime scene.

It is doubtful whether any of this had any real, longstanding harmful impact on the inquiry though.

The circumstances were unique. No cameras, no eye-witnesses, no noises, no murder weapon, no suspicious behaviour at the scene prior to the crime; this would be a tough one for any TV sleuth to solve swiftly. I think it would be unfair to apportion blame to either the French or British detectives. They have certainly devoted huge resources to this investigation.

Even one year after the massacre, the number of police documents ran to cubic metres. In a press conference given exactly one year after the bodies were discovered Monsieur Maillaud detailed some startling statistics. He said French police had spoken to 800 witnesses and taken at least 3,000 statements. Meanwhile British police said they had 560 statements. In the UK there were 1,600 evidence exhibits and 1,300 reports resulting from 2,000 "actions". Lines of inquiry were being pursued in a total of 23 different countries. By the two-year anniversary, the figures were undoubtedly more considerable still. Activity is continuing on both sides of the Channel and around the world.

It has been reported that the relationship between the French and British teams has been strained at times, but the prosecutor insists this is not so.

"Of course it is more complicated in Britain with the right to remain silent; the possibility of keeping quiet is a lot stronger in Britain," he said. "There is no point in hearing someone say 'no comment' for several hours. This is of course part of the charm and the difficulty of an international investigation. We have to juggle these different systems and respect the different procedures. Thank goodness there are European accords which allow us to work together. It is still working very well with Surrey Police. We wouldn't be able to do anything without them. It is an extraordinary team. In France there is a core group of about ten detectives, and I think there are about the same number in Surrey. They are working permanently on this case, which is very unusual after two and a half years. The longer this goes on, the fewer investigators are required. At the beginning we needed a lot of people to interview witnesses, anyone who might have heard the gunfire for example, or the motorcycle going past."

"The more time that passes, the harder it is to solve this crime," Monsieur Maillaud has previously said, but the resolve is there. Even if it takes a decade, or more, he is determined to find a resolution.

"Murders being solved 20 years after they happened

are not that unusual," he said to me in his office. "Two-and-a-half years is not that unusual. There are hundreds of unsolved murders in both France and Great Britain, and that is without even taking into account missing persons cases. Murders like this, with so many possible lines of enquiry, are rare though. We have had several in this region resolved several years later. We will never stop looking, even if we reduce the number of investigators. What is complicated is that you amass so much information, but you don't start from the beginning every day. You summarise, and in a summary there can always be an error. It's always possible we could miss something; we are all human. Even if we think everyone is doing their best it is always possible to make a mistake, or follow a wrong line of inquiry."

Rarely do police admit they might never find the killer, but that has happened with the Chevaline murders. It is a nightmare scenario for the friends and family of both the al-Hillis and Sylvain Mollier, all under such strain in the seemingly never-ending police inquiry. It is what still makes this, in Monsieur Maillaud's own soundbite, "the perfect crime"

Chapter 23

The Chevaline orphans' secret life

Most of this book has focused on the crime itself, the massacre in the French Alps which shocked so many across Europe and further afield. But the last word should be for the orphaned victims, Zainab and Zeena al-Hilli. Nor should Sylvain Mollier's three sons Leo, 18, Mathis, 15 – both from his marriage to Lydie – and Louis, three in 2015, from his relationship with Claire Schutz, be forgotten.

Zainab turned 10 in March 2015. Who knows how she celebrated that milestone birthday, her first in double figures. The friends she had in Claygate until the ill-fated holiday in France are distant memories for her now. She will have new friends now, a new teacher, a new bedroom with new toys, and colourful new clothes to replace those left behind in the caravan and at the family home in Surrey which had been the bedrock of all her childhood memories. Zeena was seven in April 2015. Did she enjoy a proper party with cake and friends around a long table singing "Happy Birthday" before she blew out the candles? I have no way of finding this out, and even if I did I wouldn't be able to reveal anything about the party or the identity of anyone there in case it gave away details of where the girls might be. All I can be sure of is the girls are being looked after by their aunt Fadwa al-Saffar, their mum's sister.

For many months both girls had faced an uncertain future back in Britain. After badly injured Zainab returned to the UK from the Alps, a lengthy court debate ensued while the police, social services and the family put forward their views on what would be best for them in the long term. Zeena, then five, and Zainab, then eight, lived in local authority care with a family until a High Court judge finally resolved the matter in 2013. A white foster family tended to them over this period. Fourteen months had passed, but both were still regarded as extremely vulnerable. They were said to be desperate to move in with their aunt, one of the familiar faces they needed in their terrified, bewildered and lonely condition.

Passing his judgment, Mr Justice Baker acceded to the girls' desire to return to the only family members they really knew.

"It is plainly in their interests to be brought up within their own natural family," he said. "Such a placement will sustain links with their family background and may help them over time to come to terms with their tragic loss."

The judge made the aunt and uncle Ahmed – Fadwa and mum Iqbal's brother - "special guardians" at the hearing in the court's Family Division. He went on that it was "in the interests of Zainab and Zeena to retain their existing family links and their identity as the children of their tragically deceased parents". That was why neither the local council nor the police suggested adoption would be an appropriate option for them. He commended Fadwa and Ahmed "for all that they have done, and all that they are going to do in the future, for the benefit of the girls".

"They have been described as thoughtful, patient and family-oriented," he went on, making it clear he agreed with this conclusion.

Of equal consideration in the hearing was the girls' security. None of the authorities present underestimated their vulnerability. "There remains a risk that whoever was responsible for the murders may try to harm the girls again," Mr Justice Baker affirmed.

The court guaranteed police protection wherever they went to live. Journalists were banned from revealing any details of where the girls were staying or where they went to school, which remains in place today. The publication of any information that might disclose their whereabouts is strictly forbidden.

In late 2013, Zainab and Zeena started at a new school. More than a year had gone by since they missed the start of the 2012/2013 academic year at Claygate Primary.

One can only hope that the girls are content. It is hard to find anyone who knows anything concrete about their current life, anyone who could provide a snapshot of their existence that I could write about even in the vaguest terms.

Saad's former next-door neighbour Brian Howells said he and his wife have not tried to make further contact with the girls. "We know they are being looked after," he said. "The best thing that can happen for the girls now is that they start a whole new life. I think that is their best chance. Their old life is behind them now."

Dr Zaid Alabdi, however, feels he and his wife have been cut off from Zainab and Zeena's lives. Two little girls who played in their gardens at weekends with their own children are now prevented from having any contact with them, Dr Alabdi said.

"The last time I saw Iqbal's sister was the day they were buried in the cemetery," Dr Alabdi told me. "We exchanged some emails but then she said she wanted to be left alone. She said her main concern is the girls. Every few months I email or text her: 'How are the girls?' She doesn't even respond. Iqbal and her sister are alike. They don't talk. I haven't seen the girls since. I know they are fine though."

Dr Alabdi remains one of the few people with a proper insight into the anguish the girls have endured.

"They were very attached to their parents so it was very hard for them not to see them," he said. "The youngest daughter who was hidden underneath her mum was too young to know what had happened. The eldest one recognised her aunt straightaway. At one point their aunt was talking of taking them back to Iraq with her. I said that if their dad was alive he would say they were British. Saad used to think of himself as more British than Iraqi. I said you have to respect their father's wishes. Perhaps that's why she doesn't talk to me. Now the kids are controlled by the aunt, who is a very closed person. My wife endlessly tries to speak with her but she doesn't answer."

James Mathews feels similarly cut off from his friend's daughters, for whom he had an intense fondness because of the experiences he and Saad shared watching their children grow up together. He has been prevented from sending gifts to Zainab, something which pains him greatly.

"Zainab never went anywhere without her favourite fluffy toy," he told me. "She used to love a little stuffed penguin. After the murders I wanted the family liaison officer to give one to her but I was told that was not possible. At one point, myself and several other friends of Saad wanted to put ourselves forward to look after the girls, but we couldn't do that either."

It is impossible to verify these claims. The authorities will not discuss anything to do with the girls.

Meanwhile, Zainab and Zeena receive all the help they could need to rebuild their shattered childhoods. Zainab has given the police as much information as she can, and specially trained family liaison officers are no doubt very careful not to disrupt her rehabilitation. It is frustrating for the investigators, but they can do little more. Their only witness is not someone with whom they can spend a week in an interview room going over every moment until a chink of light emerges through the darkness.

"Zainab says she think she saw a silhouette, but she has not given more detail than that," prosecutor Eric Maillaud told me. "Nothing that she saw at the scene has been really helpful. We can think that there was a single killer, but that does not mean there was someone else a bit further away or nearby. She does not give more detail. The psychologists who interviewed her are convinced that her brain registered what happened but for the time being she is not in a condition to express that. The brain has an ability to block memories of events that are too traumatic. They have said that what she remembers now will not enable us to solve this investigation. In a few years she might be able to remember more clearly. The problem is that when she is an adult she might read so much about her parents' deaths that it will become difficult to separate what is remembered and what is a reconstruction."

With ten detectives on both sides of the Channel still working full-time on the case, it is unlikely Zainab and Zeena will ever be forgotten about. As Dr Zaid Alabdi said to me: "In a strange way they are lucky victims because there is so much focus on them. It's like the Madeleine McCann case. They will never say it's too expensive."

Until the perpetrator is caught the two orphaned girls will for ever live in the shadow of the Chevaline murders. For them it was a crime that was anything but perfect. For them, that meticulously planned mass execution was the end of childhood innocence and the start of a nightmare which will haunt them for the rest of their days.

ABOUT THE AUTHOR

Tom Parry is the Daily Mirror's Senior Feature Writer and one of its longest-serving foreign correspondents. He won the Feature Writer of the Year category at the 2014 Press Awards for his articles on the Ebola crisis in Liberia, the 70th anniversary of D-Day and the illegal ivory trade in Kenya.

It was the third year in succession he had been shortlisted. Previously Tom has been one of only three nominees put forward for Italy's prestigious Dario d'Angelo Award for his series on freed child soldiers in Uganda.

A fluent French speaker, Tom has covered many of the major news events in France in recent years, including the al-Hilli murders.

He is also the author of Thumbs Up Australia, a critically acclaimed travel book about his time hitchhiking through the Outback.

A dad's heartbreaking account of his treasured daughter's life that was cut short in a horrific honeymoon murder